HIDE!
HERE COMES THE
INSURANCE GUY

D1562772

HIDE!

HERE COMES THE INSURANCE GUY

Understanding Business Insurance
and Risk Management

Rick Vassar

CPCU, ARM, AIS, ARM-P

iUniverse, Inc.
New York   Bloomington

Hide! Here Comes the Insurance Guy

Understanding Business Insurance and Risk Management

iUniverse Star
an iUniverse, Inc. imprint

iUniverse books may be ordered through booksellers or by contacting:

iUniverse
1663 Liberty Drive
Bloomington, IN 47403
www.iuniverse.com
1-800-Authors (1-800-288-4677)

ISBN: 978-1-60528-020-2 (pbk)
ISBN: 978-0-595-49811-6 (cloth)
ISBN: 978-0-595-61492-9 (ebk)

Printed in the United States of America

To Carol, my one and only

"Discretion will protect you, and understanding will guard you."
—Proverbs 2:11

Quotes and Reviews

Hide! Here Comes the Insurance Guy

Seasoned insurance professionals, especially those who cannot explain policy terms to clients without using dizzying industry lingo, will find "Hide! Here Comes the Insurance Guy" particularly digestible, detailed and delightful.

- David Dankwa, Senior Associate Editor, BestWeek

I found this book to be an excellent tool for the insurance novice and expert alike, and I would recommend it for both consumers and the business community. The insights Vassar offers into the risk management process are invaluable, and the material is written in an easy-to-read, approachable format.

- Dr. George L. Head Ph.D., CPCU, ARM, CSP, CLU, Director Emeritus, American Institute for Chartered Property Casualty Underwriters (Ret.)

...Vassar's focus is practical and hands-on, leavened with a self-deprecating sense of humor. Did I say "humor"? Yes, though few comedy clubs are likely to feature an Open Mike night for insurance reps, Vassar takes the human antipathy toward insurance and turns it into a source of mirth and amusement.

- Kevin M. Quinley CPCU, ARM, AIC, Are, AIM, Author, Business At Risk

If you're going to get past being small service business owner, you have to learn the basics of how insurance works. You probably won't have time to become an expert on insurance (although I tried) but Hide! Here Comes the Insurance Guy and Rick Vassar will give you the basic understanding that you need.

- Jeffery T. Valcourt, Chairman, Valcourt Building Services

This book is highly recommended for any business owner or executive responsible for procuring insurance or managing claims or litigation for the business. Almost as good as the fact that it packs a great deal of information into a readable format is that this book is actually funny.

- Eric Kaidanow, Esq., Frontier Risk Management

The Envelope, please … the Top Risk Management Book of the Year …

By Kevin M. Quinley CPCU, ARM AIC, AIM, ARe

"Olly olly oxen free! Come out, come out, wherever you are!"
Reviewed by Kevin Quinley

Hide! Here Comes the Insurance Guy by Rick Vassar, iUniverse, 2006, 196 pp., $17.95

Somebody once said that a New York accent was the most effective form of birth control known to man. Others might nominate as an effective contraceptive any tendency to talk about insurance… or risk management, for that matter.

Author, risk manager and consultant Rick Vassar has penned an illuminating primer on insurance and risk management in his book, "Hide! Here Comes the Insurance Guy." The title is a take-off on the notion that, for most people, meeting with an insurance person or discussing coverage is as much fun as a root canal or proctological exam. The author – a CPCU and an ARM -- lives a dual existence. By day, he is a mild-mannered risk manager for a company in the Washington D.C. area. In his spare time, he writes and consults on risk management topics (check out http://www.vassargroup.com). Vassar tries (successfully) to cushion the blow and counter the stereotype by presenting insurance and risk management principles in a straightforward way that can profit any business professional.

Part of his theme is that most companies have risks that are overseen by someone whose title is not "Risk Manager." Most companies do not have risk managers; you need to have a pretty big insurance budget to justify that as a full-time position. No company vies to be paying so much in insurance premium that they spotlight the problem by having a full-time individual to tend to it. Nevertheless, all companies have risks and need to manage it. For these risk managers without title or formal portfolio, Vassar's book – perhaps the best risk management book of the year even without that phrase in the title -- is an indispensable primer and guide. Reading and heeding his advice will save businesses much money, frustration and Excedrin-consumption.

Vassar divides his book into three main sections. Part I discusses business strategies to even the playing field between policyholders and insurance companies. Part II walks through the major basic forms of insurance coverage for most any business. Part III rounds out with a useful; glossary and index.

Vassar's target audience is likely not the Fortune 500 or Fortune 1000 risk pro who attends the annual RIMS Conference. There is no highfalutin discussion of enterprise risk management or views from 50,000 feet above ground level. If you are seeking information on Sarbanes-Oxley compliance or the risk management implications of global warming, look elsewhere. The storefront risk manager, though, will find a wellspring of effective tips and tricks between these covers.

Vassar's focus is practical and hands-on, leavened with a self-deprecating sense of humor. Did I say "humor"? Yes, though few comedy clubs are likely to feature an Open Mike night for insurance reps, Vassar takes the human antipathy toward insurance and turns it into a source of mirth and amusement. (Some end-of-chapter checklists would have been a nice addition to the text, but this is a minor quibble.)

So run -- but don't hide - and get your copy of "Hide! Here Comes the Insurance Guy." Get out from under the desk. Leave the closet and face your fears. Insurance and risk management may not be fun (though they are occasionally funny), but Rick Vassar has come as close to anyone in blending sharp wit with moneysaving risk management insights.

Kevin Quinley CPCU ARM is the author of over 500 published articles and nine books. His articles have appeared in publications including Business Insurance, The National Underwriter, Risk Management, Occupational Safety & Health, Best's Review, CPCU Journal, Insurance Settlement Journal, The Risk Report and For the Defense. He is the author of Time Management for Claim Professionals, Claim Management, The Quality Plan, Litigation Management and Winning Strategies for Negotiating Claims and Managing Product Liability Risks. His seventh book, Bulletproofing Your Medical Practice: Risk Management Strategies that Work, was published in October of 2000. His eighth book, Well-Adjusted: 185 Career Tips for Adjuster Success was published in mid-2001. The ninth book – coauthored with Don Schmidt -- Business at Risk: Risk Managing the Terrorist Threat was published in 2002.

Book Review: Hide, Here Comes the Insurance Guy
Written by MaryAnna Clemons
Published August 22, 2007

Rick Vassar has found a niche subject (business risk insurance) that was lacking in coverage, so he wrote the book on it. And he did a great job doing it. The book, Hide, Here Comes the Insurance Guy; A Practical Guide to Understanding Business Insurance and Risk Management, is a job well done.

We all have to buy insurance for our cars, our homes, even our lives. But business insurance is a totally different animal. If you run a business, you have to have insurance. It's that simple.

Rick spells out what that insurance is, why you need it and why you'll be sorry if you don't have it. He has demystified more than a few insurance terms, opened up the world of risk (and the risk is all yours without insurance) and given compelling case scenarios to show what can happen without insurance.

If I had to pick on something to critique, I'd say that some of his headlines don't seem to match his later words, for example "Why people hate insurance" is the headline and then the anecdote that follows is about algebra. I would argue that people hate insurance because they pay and pay and pay and pay, and then finally, they submit a claim and they get hassled and hassled and hassled, until they finally settle for less than they should be getting from an insurance company. To me, that's why people hate insurance.

I think, though, that Rick was tying Algebra — the subject everyone thinks they'll never need --- into insurance, because at some point in life you'll need both. That is a pretty picky critique on my part, because nothing is perfect.

Back to the good stuff, I really like the way Rick has broken it down for you on the ins and outs of the insurance game. For one, he tells you to get more than one quote - at first that seems like common sense, but when was the last time you got a quote?

I had to think about it and for my car insurance, it's been at least four years. How would I know if I'm getting the best rate if I haven't bothered to shop around in four years? Nice reminder to me.

The same applies for business insurance and going through a broker. The broker is in business for himself or his company, not you. You are the payee and if you aren't paying, they don't make money, which is just part of the reason your insurance rates tend to go up every year, instead of down.

The book breaks down the claims process, defines your risk criteria, gives you the difference between self-insurance and no-insurance (personal alternative risk financing), brokers, lawyers and more.

When you are done reading this book you are going to understand:

The language of insurance
The insurance players who want your money
How to develop a sound insurance strategy
How to invest your time and efforts regarding insurance
And whether you are properly insured or not

Part two of the book is worth the cover price alone: Insurance 101. In this section Rick breaks down the different insurance policies, from cars to homes to worker's compensation: what is covered, what isn't, what you can expect from your insurance, time periods, and more.

Worker's Compensation 101: worker's compensation is mandatory in all states, but Rick explains that small businesses, based on the number of employees, can file for exemptions. He then goes on to explain why you may not want to do that. After all, even if you have two employees, if both of those employees get hurt, you aren't covered (let the lawsuits begin). Even if you think that your cousin Fred would never sue you, or that he won't get hurt because he's super-athletic, think again. Accidents (and fraud) do happen, even with friends and family.

Rick's enduring message through the whole book (174 pages, including Index) is to protect yourself and your business with insurance, while protecting your pocketbook from the insurance man. It's a great book and I'm glad I have it on my business reference shelf.

Since the book is published by iUniverse, I'll take moment to point out that it's very well edited. The book has a great binding that I've been bending, pulling and adjusting on and it's stuck together wonderfully. I would not be surprised to find this book as required reading in future business courses in colleges throughout the U.S. and for new insurance agents to give to their clients (smart marketing in action: educate the customer). The layout is professional and easy on the eyes.

As an avid book reader and buyer, I tend to shy away from self-published work - I'm glad I did not in this case. It's a well done book that hands you information to make your life easier.

MaryAnna Clemons is a freelance journalist based out of Colorado Springs, Colo., with three children, five horses, five cats, five dogs and one husband. Writing about removing chemicals from our daily lives, the dangers of aspartame and vaccines, as well as book reviews, she is continually trying to cram as much writing into her day as she can.

In New Book, Risk Manager Explains 'Commercial Insurance' in Plain Language

OLDWICK, N.J. November 13 (BestWire) — "If I had grown up in Wisconsin, I would know cheese; Georgia, peaches; Florida, AARP," writes risk manager and author Rick Vassar.

As fate would have it, Vassar was raised in a suburb of Hartford, Conn., the insurance capital of the world, where "folks gather at the local diner in the center of town and discuss such compelling subjects as the necessity of waiver of subrogation and additional insured status or the effects the new insurance commissioner would have on the local economy."

This is where "the insurance curse began in my family," he writes.

In his book, "Hide! Here Comes the Insurance Guy," described as a practical guide to understanding business insurance and risk management, Vassar shares the wealth of information he's gathered over several decades in what he calls "plain speaking" insurance language.

There aren't any books available that address the needs of the business insurance consumer, and second, many business professionals refuse to enlighten themselves on the nuances of the insurance trade, he says. As such, "the insurance guy" Vassar describes in his book is a lonely person, something of a corporate outcast. He is the type of co-worker people steer away from in the hallways, afraid that he'd work insurance into a conversation.

Using humor, Vassar, also founder and president of Virginia-based Vassar Group, provides insight into the commercial insurance industry from a risk manager's perspective, offering practical advice on the insurance purchasing process. As he describes how terrorism insurance works, how to value one's property when considering property coverage, and workers' compensation strategies, he also picks on attorneys in a section called "The Skinny on Attorneys" and on adjusters in "Anatomy of an Insurance Adjuster."

Vassar discusses in depth the selection of an insurance broker and argues that bigger isn't always better. The difference between a big, national broker and a local or regional broker is like Advil and Ibuprofen, he writes. "You're only paying extra for the name."

Vassar says if a company is in tune with what's going on in the marketplace, it can get the same pricing from a small local broker that would from a midsize, regional broker or Marsh & McLennan.

Also, from a service standpoint, Vassar says he prefers a midsize broker to handle his company's midsize account. "Currently, we have a good bit of premium but it wouldn't be a big number for a national broker, like Marsh. For a midsize broker, it's a significant portion of their overall book of business. So, we're more of a big fish in a small pond, whereas with a bigger national firm, we wouldn't get the same level of service," he says.

He frowns on the practice of corporate insureds assigning brokers to shop specific markets, often at the urging of the incumbent broker who insists that "the underwriter only wants to work with one broker per account." Vassar writes that assigning markets defeats the purpose of a free-market system.

He writes also about the role of lawyers in claims processing. "If you're an organization, especially in a self-insured or self-funding situation and you're going to make a decision that's going to have a financial impact on your company, then it needs to be the company that is making the decision as to the financial viability of either settling the case or taking it to trial. Many companies just hand it off to lawyers as soon as they get a lawsuit."

Vassar cites the McDonald's hot coffee case, "where there was an opportunity to settle the case as a medical claim, and they ignored it. Well, the issues in that case were that there was a legitimate injury, a legitimate burn, and eventually they did work to improve the cups and they lowered the temperature of the coffee that they were serving. They also later settled the claim for a much higher amount."

While the book targets buyers of insurance, Vassar says the insurance community also can learn a lot from it. "I believe the book will give valuable insight to the insurance community as to how risk managers and businesses process their information concerning risk and insurance. If a broker or insurer has a better understanding of the needs and concerns of the insured, they will be better able to market products that will meet these needs."

And what do businesses need? Vassar says it is: "The best price and the comfort of knowing that what they are buying will cover an event that creates a financial uncertainty which could prevent them from opening their doors tomorrow, or could close their doors forever."

By David Dankwa, associate editor, BestWeek: David.Dankwa@ambest.com

Contents

Introduction   xiii

Acknowledgments   xvii

Part I   *Business Insurance Strategies to Even the Playing Field*

CHAPTER 1   Who Is the Insurance Guy?   3

So How Does One Go About Becoming a RiskManager?   3

Don't Ask Me How I Know   6

The Risk Manager   7

The Lonely Guy   9

How This Book Will Save You Money   10

The Insurance Guy   11

Why People Hate Insurance   12

CHAPTER 2   Insurance, the Necessary Evil   14

Your First Brush with Business Insurance   14

The Business Gets Going   16

The Business Really Gets Going   17

Why So Many Businesses Consider Insurance a Necessary Evil   17

The Baffle Factor   20

It's All about the Cash   22

Frequently Asked Questions   22

CHAPTER 3   What the Heck Is Risk Management?   29

The Evolution of Risk Management   29

The Gramm-Leach-Bliley Act (1999)   32

The Risk-Management Process   32

The ABCs of the Risk-Management Process   33

Action Plan   34

Am I a Risk Manager Yet?   36

CHAPTER 4   Brokers   38

Friends, Compatriots, or Über-Salespeople   38

How Did Your Last Insurance Renewal Go?   39

Keep All Your Marbles in One Sack   41

Not Just Any Broker   42

The Broker Relationship   43

When Things Get Rough, Go Shopping 44

How to Market Your Insurance Program 45

Pricing 48

A Proactive Approach 49

CHAPTER 5   What's the Deal with Lawyers? 50

Why Lawsuits Can Get Out of Hand 50

"We Can Win This Thing" 51

Controlling the Direction of the Case 51

The Lesson 52

The Lessons Learned 54

The Skinny on Attorneys 58

CHAPTER 6   Do You Hate Claims As Much As I Do? 59

A Sobering Reality 59

Strategies to Help You Along 62

Anatomy of an Insurance Adjuster 64

A Day in the Life 65

Fred 67

Breaking Down the Claim Package 68

Why Everyone Loves Collection Agencies 71

It's All in How You Relate 73

CHAPTER 7   Self-Insurance/No Insurance —
What's the Difference? 74

Alternative Risk Financing 74

To Most People, Self-Insurance Is No Insurance 75

The Bad News 76

Reinsurance—It's Kind of Like Booking a Bet 78

Personal Alternative Risk Financing 79

Business Alternative Risk Financing 80

Top-Down Commitment to Self-Funding of Claims 81

Retrospectively Rated Insurance Plans 82

Deductible Programs 83

Self-Insured Retention (SIR) Programs 85

Hiring an Adjusting Company 85

Structuring the SIR Is the Key 89

If You Go Out, Stay Out! 90

Familiar Ground 91

CHAPTER 8   The Power of Positive Audit Experiences 93

What You Don't Know about the Audit Process Can Hurt You 93

An Auditor's Ultimate Goal   94
The Results Are in the Preparation   96
Workers' Compensation Audits   96
Leveling the Playing Field   97
If Your Renewal Date Is January 1, Move It!   98
General Liability Audits   99
Automobile Audits   100
The Significance of Audit Planning   100
The Appeal Process   101

PART II   *Understanding Your Insurance Policies*

CHAPTER 9   Insurance 101 —Automobile Liability   105
Your Company's Single Most Important Risk   105
It's All about Control (or Lack Thereof)   106
Types of Commercial Auto Policies   106
Auto Liability Coverage Explained   108
Why Not Use the Scheduled and Composite Policies Together?   111
What If the Bank Holds the Note?   111
Driver Approval   111
Using the Drug-Free Workplace to Qualify the Drivers   112
The Named Driver Policy   113

CHAPTER 10   Insurance 101 — Property/ Package Coverage 114
Why Do I Have to Insure Packages?   114
What You Really Need to Know about Property   115
Your Owned Property Risk Analysis   115
Valuing Your Property   116
That Coinsurance Thing   116
Let the Insurance Company Value the Property   118
Real Property versus Personal Property   119

CHAPTER 11   Insurance 101 —General Liability   122
A Road Map   122
General Liability—What It Covers   122
Structure of the General Liability Policy   123
Auditable Policy   124
Covered, Excluded = Product   126
Commercial General Liability—Got to Have It   127

CHAPTER 12 Insurance 101 —Workers' Compensation   129

It's Mandatory, Even When It Isn't   129
Fraud in Workers' Compensation Claims   130
Classification of Employees   131
The Scopes Manual   132
Premium Calculation   132
The Experience Modification (EMR), or "Mod Rate"   132
Workers' Compensation Strategies   133
Miscellaneous Provisions within the Work Comp Policy   134

CHAPTER 13 Insurance 101 —
Miscellaneous Insurance Coverage   136

Umbrella, EPLI, D&O, E&O, and Environmental   136
Miscellaneous Insurance Coverage   138
Umbrella Liability   139
Professional/Errors and Omissions (E&O) Liability   140
Employment Practices Liability (EPLI)   140
Directors and Officers (D&O) Coverage   142
Crime Policy   142
Environmental Liability   143
Disclaimer   143

CHAPTER 14 How to Talk Insurance Like You Know
What You're Talking About   145

How to Sound Like an Insurance Pro   145
The Myth of the Hard Market   145
Terrorism Risk Insurance Act (TRIA) of 2002   148
Tort Reform   148
Lawyers!   149
Conclusion   151

Part III   Terms to Know

Glossary   155
Index   167

Introduction

The first thing people ask me about this book is: "Why a book on insurance? And business insurance, to boot?" To me, this question really means: "You're kidding, right?" In fact, when I initially pitched this idea to the publisher, I was met with an uncomfortable silence on the other end of the line. Fortunately, being in the insurance end of business, I'm pretty accustomed to stunned silence.

After about five seconds of this, I gave it my best marketing effort:

"Sounds kind of like death, doesn't it?"

The reason for this book is simple. There are too few insurance professionals who work outside of the insurance industry. The insurance industry is a wonderful career choice for those who pursue it and stay with it. Most who go into this line of business stay in the business until they retire—or die.

I am an anomaly in the insurance industry. I have spent my entire career in business and not in insurance. I am not a purveyor of insurance; I am a consumer of insurance.

I am a risk manager.

A risk manager determines the financing needs of an organization, provides coverage for the company, and works the insurance program on behalf of his or her employer.

I am a buyer, not a seller. I look out for the needs of the commercial consumer, and I have no ties to the insurance industry other than as a consumer. At no time have I ever worked in the supply side of insurance.

On the other hand, the insurance industry has certified me as an expert in the property casualty field, conferring on me four professional insurance designations (certifications) including the Chartered Property Casualty Underwriter (CPCU), which is considered the gold standard in the property/casualty insurance industry.

I am not saying this to toot my own horn but to point out that I have always represented the interests of the business consumer, whether a sole proprietorship or a Fortune 100 company.

Yet there are precious few of us who have remained untouched by the supply end of the insurance food chain. Most, if not all, of the information that is communicated concerning business insurance is generated by the insurance industry itself.

I remember when I fell into the risk-management role at the company I was working for at the time. I almost had a nervous breakdown. Was it because of the pressure of handling insurance for the entire organization? Or was it because that same year, the company had decided to self-insure its entire fleet of vehicles—about 5,000 vehicles?

Nope. It was because I couldn't understand a single word they were saying!

And although I was completely lost, I didn't want anyone to know that I was pretty much a fraud. The insurance professionals knew better, though. And they were circling hard.

I was able to get my hands on a little book on insurance made simple. I'm pretty sure it was a generic insurance book more geared to personal insurance than business insurance, but it was definitely written from an industry perspective.

All I can remember from the book was that it was about eighty pages long, but it contained twelve pages on bailment. Bailment! For you nonlawyers out there, bailment is the act of placing property into the custody and control of another, who is responsible for returning the property in the same condition. Reading that book, you would have thought that bailment was central to the insurance universe. In the past fifteen years, I have probably had five situations arise that dealt with the issue of bailment. And I worked for a car rental company!

When I looked at the marketplace, there was nothing on the subject of business insurance from the business perspective—nothing! So this is where we'll start.

There are four distinct steps to controlling and then improving your insurance costs:

1. *Understand the language.* Like any other specialization, insurance has a language and cadence all its own. You must learn the language to understand the process.

2. *Know the players.* Once you understand how all the pieces fit together, you will better understand the process. Better understanding leads to better management, which leads to savings.

3. *Develop a strategy.* Just as your business has a game plan (for example goals, vision, mission, five-year plan), there are subtle yet distinct ways to work your insurance program to maximize your coverage for minimal cost.

4. *Invest the time.* You spend years and years going to school so you can get a good job or start your own business. You go to conferences and seminars to aid in your development as your career progresses. If you take the time initially to learn about insurance, how it works, and how you can make it work for you, it will help you reap real financial benefits while providing the maximum coverage for your company.

This is what the Insurance Guy series is all about: simple explanations, practical solutions, and time-tested strategies that will reap huge savings in insurance costs.

Real numbers. Real solutions.

As you read through this book, you will find that it is mapped out to be used not just as an initial learning tool but also as an ongoing resource, when issues arise in your insurance program that may not have been as important when you first read the book.

The first section is an overview of business insurance, with practical solutions and strategies for improving your program, cutting your costs, and increasing the value of the program, which, in turn, increases the value of your company. It explains how to deal with brokers, lawyers, claims adjusters, auditors, and other players in the insurance industry. It digs below the surface not only to show how to approach these situations, but also to relate personal examples that demonstrate why these strategies are effective.

The second section explains the most basic insurance coverage, such as workers' compensation, general liability, and auto liability, as well as some popular miscellaneous coverage, including employment practices liability, environmental, and directors and officers, to name a few. This section is valuable when you actually sit down with a policy. Since all policies are essentially the same in structure, you can use this section as a resource to give you a simple explanation of how the policy and coverage all fit together.

The third section is the glossary. Words and phrases that are in parentheses throughout the book are included alphabetically in the glossary. This is like having a French/English dictionary while touring Paris. You kind of know French, but when they start talking fast, you sometimes need to go to the book to remember what a word or phrase means. The glossary can serve as a quick reference when you just don't know what those insurance people are talking about. By utilizing the sections alone or in tandem, you will be able to develop a viable strategy that will lead to real cost savings.

I have tried to communicate this information in an entertaining manner. You will see, though, that the humor is there to set up a point. I do not intend to denigrate or diminish any aspect of the insurance industry in any way. Humor has helped, through the years, to make insurance a little more palatable to me—a spoonful of sugar, as they say.

And if anyone out there should take offense at any of my views, please observe that I see myself through a more critical eye than I do the insurance industry.

I hope you enjoy reading this as much as I have enjoyed writing it. It is my desire to shorten the learning curve for you, the reader, and to fill in the blanks of your business insurance education.

Rick Vassar

Acknowledgments

Thanks to John Woodall, Jim Chambers, Art Cifci, Morris Kletzkin, Greg Young, Perry Ballard, and Jim Misselwitz for being in my corner no matter what. Special thanks to Pete Lafley, Burke O'Malley, and Jeff Valcourt for giving me a chance when chances were hard to come by.

Cover illustration by Laura Dreyer.

PART I

Business Insurance Strategies to Even the Playing Field

My dad used to umpire baseball and referee football. For as long as I can remember, he would spend almost every weekend from March through November on a college campus. Sometimes he was popular, sometimes not. That's how it goes in the officiating business.

Accompanying my dad to those games were some of the best memories I have of my childhood. With Mom not around, he would take the time to explain how life worked and how sports related to life and life to sports.

He used to tell me that when umpiring baseball it was 90 percent instinct and 10 percent rules. In football, it was 90 percent rules and 10 percent instinct. He would say how he liked football, but he loved baseball because he had to rely more on his instincts.

In business, there are rules as well. Yet the most successful business people rely most on their instincts when it comes to making tough decisions. That gut feeling and the willingness to go with that feeling make the difference between wild success, quiet desperation, and total failure.

Insurance is no different. Most businesspeople, though, don't trust their instincts enough when it comes to insurance, because they lack the knowledge to take those kinds of risks.

Business insurance is also no different. There are rules, but there are also decisions that can be made based on what's in the gut.

This section will provide you with strategies that you can apply to your business. It will give you the knowledge and understanding to make informed insurance decisions without relying on an outside expert. If you apply these strategies, you will have enough information to be able to go with your gut.

Insurance is probably 80 percent rules and 20 percent instinct. It's that 20 percent that will allow you to realize significant savings in your organization's insurance program and, in turn, to increase the value of your product or service as well as the overall value of the company.

1
Who Is the Insurance Guy?

So How Does One Go About Becoming a Risk Manager?

I guess I've always had a bent toward managing risk. And when I was young, my mom worked from the same book as every other mom. She would tell me not to do this because I would poke somebody's eye out or not to do that because my face would freeze that way—one part Dr. Spock and two parts Dr. Seuss.

The first "momism" I ever questioned was the clean underwear rationale. Now, like all other kids under the age of ten, I believed that if you didn't bathe, there was no need to change your underwear, contrary to the prevailing parental handbook at the time. So my mom would use the example that all moms used, right from the handbook:

"What if you got into an accident? Do you want to have dirty underwear on when the ambulance shows up? I don't think so."

Well, even at the tender age of ten, I found fault with this reasoning:

1. If I were to be in an accident that required a trip in an ambulance, I would much prefer that the paramedics waive the inspection of my undergarments and concentrate on getting me to the hospital, instead.

2. If I saw a tractor trailer coming at me at fifty miles per hour, it would be more than a safe bet that I would soil something out of sheer terror. It would only be a matter of whether it would happen prior to or after the accident.

In my mother's defense, though, I must admit that I did once poke myself in the eye while running with a sharpened pencil, so I can personally attest to that advice. At the age of ten though, I was already looking for the angle.

Today, I look at all the angles, and this is the basis of managing risk.

It turns out that my mother worked for a life insurance company a couple of lifetimes ago, and she is very interested in the insurance industry and the nuances of insurance laws, philosophy, and contracts. This is probably where the insurance curse began in my family.

I also grew up in a suburb of Hartford, Connecticut, which is known as the "Insurance Capital of the World." If I had grown up in Wisconsin, I would know cheese; Georgia, peaches; Florida, AARP. In the Hartford area, folks would gather at the local diner in the center of town and discuss such compelling subjects as the necessity of waiver of subrogation and additional insured status or the effects the new insurance commissioner would have on the local economy. By the way, the second biggest seller in the Hartford area is coffee.

One of the first lessons I learned about insurance in a small business came in 1984. I was a branch manager for an independently owned car rental company with six branches. I received a call from a customer who indicated that she had rear-ended another vehicle and that one of the passengers might be hurt—but not too badly. Since our vehicle was drivable, I asked her to fill out an accident report when she returned.

As I drove in the next morning, I saw the vehicle on the lot. Since I was not there when the customer returned the vehicle, I asked my assistant manager if she had filled out a report. "Oh sure, here it is," she answered. On the report was the name of the customer, her phone number, and the name of the other party involved. I guess she couldn't be bothered with the rest of the form.

I spoke to my boss later that day and asked him if I should call the customer to get some more information before I turned in the accident report to the insurance company.

"Naw, don't worry about it," he told me. "We pay those insurance people so much money; let 'em earn it. As a matter of fact, let's see if the other folks call us, and then we'll turn it in."

Of course, we did hear from the other party, about six months later, when a letter of representation arrived from the other party's lawyer. At that point, we sent the little bit of information we had to our insurance carrier. This left them six months behind in defending the claim. The involvement of the attorney, which might have been avoided if we had reported the claim earlier, increased the amount of the claim as well.

I never found out how that claim was resolved, but a little over two years later, the car rental company was in bankruptcy, and the organization did not survive. This was not a direct result of poor claims administration but rather the result of ignorance and/or unwillingness to pay attention to the details of business.

In a struggling organization, though, paying attention to your insurance program can be the difference between survival and failure.

I have met so many intelligent, hardworking, and innovative people over the years, people who started businesses in their basements and were able to develop them into multilevel functional companies that turn profits year in and year out.

I have also seen small businesses that grow in the first few years, only to falter and fail while attempting to make the transition from a mom-and-pop operation to the big time. Oftentimes, this is due to a company's inability to highlight and enhance its strengths while supplementing its resources in key areas.

If you polled businesspeople throughout the United States and even the world and asked which core area of their business is the least understood and least likely to be of interest to them, the answer would be overwhelmingly, "Insurance! Insurance! Insurance!"

In the olden days (that's what my daughter calls the 1960s), pollsters used to go door-to-door asking questions. Let's imagine the scene: a pollster knocks on the door; a lady in curlers answers.

The pollster asks, "Ma'am, I'd like to ask what you think is the greatest problem in the country today—ignorance or apathy?"

The lady answers, "I don't know, and I don't care!"

General liability, experience mod rates, retro plans, reinsurance—most executives do not have the time or the inclination to learn about all the vagaries of insurance, so they rely on others from outside the company to determine the insurance needs of the organization. Brokers, agents, and loss control representatives probably dictate the coverage you need to run your business. And yet all those people profit from the products they advise or compel your business to buy.

This book will not attempt to re-explain the unexplainable aspects of insurance. Instead, I will give you, the reader, the basic knowledge to understand your needs, to manage the risks you take every day when you open your doors for business, and to determine what you need to protect your assets and your operations cost-effectively.

Information you can use; strategies you can use.

The savings are there. You just need a map to show you where to find them.

Most executives will nod knowingly as the details are spelled out. But I have found it quite difficult to hold the attention of, well, anyone, when the subject turns to insurance. They start off interested, but in a very short time, their minds start to drift to that place where no one else has ever been.

And you can never get them back—at least not as long as you are still talking about insurance.

✗ There is a technical term for this in the insurance industry—"eyes glazed over," which is different than the look you get when you give an executive bad news about a big claim. The industry term for that is "deer in headlights."

When you attempt to educate people about insurance, it is imperative to get to the point as soon as possible before the mind begins to freeze, at which time all transfer of information will cease.

So, here goes. This is not intended to be a comprehensive treatise on the insurance industry, but rather a commonsense guide that will present the knowledge and strategies that are effective in the boardroom as well as the back room.

You will also find various insurance words and phrases in parentheses throughout this book. If you learn what each of these phrases means in the context of the insurance industry, you will be able to talk your way through many a conversation with insurance professionals who may truly believe that you know what you're talking about. You will find these phrases listed alphabetically in the glossary, each with a short definition so you can use the glossary as a quick reference guide, should a particular term baffle you.

Don't Ask Me How I Know

I was driving in my car the other day when I heard a line in some old country song that made me laugh out loud. It was a guy warning someone, probably a younger person, not to do certain things when confronted with decisions in his or her life. Each verse ended with the phrase "Don't ask me how I know," implying that the singer had made these mistakes and learned from them.

Let me give you some of my own examples:

A six-year-old boy runs up to his mom with his hands cupped, holding a pile of dog poop, and says, "Hey, Mom, look what I almost stepped in!"

Don't ask me how I know.

If you are in a snowball fight, never ever aim at the big guy with the bad temper, especially if he's faster than you.

When your buddy gives you a bottle of wine called Southern Comfort, check the proof before you take a few belts.

Don't ask the rather rotund new neighbor when her baby is due.

Never attempt to fix a plumbing fixture until you are certain the water is turned off.

Don't ever drink red wine with fish or with tequila.

Don't ask me how I know.

The Risk Manager

You know me. I'm the guy who works for your company who always appears to be a little disheveled, a little distracted, and just a little bit strange.

"Hey," you might ask, "what does that guy do?"

"He's the risk manager," is the reply. "He does the insurance. Whatever you do, don't talk to him. Nobody ever talks to him. If you do, he's going to bore you with all that insurance nonsense, and since people rarely ever talk to him, he won't let you get away. Some folks say he's brilliant, but I'm not really sure. No one really knows what he's talking about, so they leave him alone. Actually, in a big company like this, that alone makes him a genius. He hangs out with the IT guy. Go figure."

I graduated from college twenty-five years ago in Washington DC as a political science major. At the time, I figured I had it made. What better place to be for a poli-sci major?

Eleven days before graduation, though, the government put a freeze on all federal hiring. This made the market for newly graduated political science majors quite a bit more competitive. (Read: nonexistent.)

So I waited tables. I also had various driving positions—bus driver for a bowling alley, delivery boy for a nuclear medicine pharmacy, courier.

So it came as no surprise that I ended up in the car rental industry. Not just the car rental industry, though—the insurance-replacement car rental industry. You know, the folks you rent from when your car is in the shop. Quitting that job three years later was one of the happiest days of my life.

It was also the greatest management experience of my life. The price for a replacement car was about half that of a vehicle rented at the airport, so this company had strict procedures for everything. Everything was budgeted, all paperwork had to be accounted for, and every minute of every day was filled up.

This job took me to exotic places such as Sacramento, California, and Baltimore, Maryland, and taught me how to manage myself and my time. I developed some good friendships along the way, and—oh yeah, *I hated every minute of it.*

I got into the retail end of car rental a few years later, thinking I had hit the big time. The only really good thing that came out of that experience is the day I met my wife, which is still *the* happiest day of my life.

Burned out at the ripe old age of twenty-six, I accepted a job running a twenty-five-car fleet in a rental office located in a strip mall. The office was on the second floor, below an OB/GYN office, so I sat staring out the window watching pregnant women come and go all day. Occasionally, a customer would show up.

A few months later, I went to lunch with my boss. This was the exchange:

Boss: We want you to continue to run your office, but you will also be a district manager overseeing three more offices. We'll give you another $50 a week. (That just about doubled my salary.)

Me: That's great.

Boss: There is a condition. We need you to take over claims for the company as well.

Me: No way! I hate claims. I will never do claims. You can't make me do claims.

Boss: We'll give you another $25 per week and a percentage of all the property damage you collect.

Me: When do I start?

So I became a claims guy. Five days later, I got a call about a company driver having rear-ended a little old lady. She called me and mailed me an estimate. I made up a release, did a check request, and went over to the accounting department to pick up the check for $221. As the controller handed me the check, she uttered the profound words that changed my professional life: "You know we have insurance for this."

I was floored. "You mean I don't have to settle claims, even though I am the 'claims manager'?" I asked.

"Nope, just turn it in to the insurance company and let them deal with it."

"Really?"

And so it went. The company grew about 300 percent in six years, and as folks quit or died, I ascended to the position of Director of Risk Management. At that time, this meant "person who did everything no one else wants to do."

On any given day, 50 percent of the managers would hate me, and 50 percent would love me. The next day, the ratio would be the same, only it wouldn't be the same managers. I would tell the not-so-friendly managers that one day they would love me, because one day they would need me. And it was true, they would.

Why?

Well, eventually, everyone experiences a car wreck of some kind. Then they would call me, making all nice and asking for help with the insurance company. I would help, and they would love me (just as I had predicted) until the claim was settled. Magically, at that point, I became a big jerk again.

Recently, I earned the Chartered Property Casualty Underwriter (CPCU) designation, the highest designation or certification for property casualty insurance professionals. Once I had passed all the requirements, I discovered some very interesting statistics.

For example, of the more than twenty-five thousand insurance professionals in the CPCU Society, less than one percent are in non-industry-related jobs. Thus, the majority of insurance experts by far are employed in the insurance industry, working for an insurance company, a broker, or another insurance-industryrelated company. There are hardly any of us insurance guys who have never held a position in the insurance industry.

The Lonely Guy

I am a lonely guy. At home, my wife and kids love me because I don't talk much about insurance there. Professionally, however, I am the loneliest guy in the world. I once called the Maytag repairman; he put me on hold and never came back.

You see, when I walk the halls, people know that if they talk to me, I may try to work insurance into the conversation. So they duck around a corner or dive under a desk. Some will even get on the phone to other departments:

"Joe? Hi. Hide, here comes the insurance guy!"

On the other hand, some brokers and insurance company employees will not take my calls because I might actually ask a question that they might not be able to answer—at least, not honestly. Then it's "Hide! Here comes 'the Insurance Guy'!" Once when I called a broker's office, I actually overheard someone in the background yelling, "If that's Rick Vassar, tell him I'm not here."

Oh, and a word of advice: if you are going to call me an evil name at the end of a telephone conversation, make sure the phone is completely disconnected when the conversation is over. And don't deny you said it when I call you back. And I *will* call you back.

The reason I can speak of such things is because I've lived it. If you have walked in my shoes, you know it to be a very lonely road. I have worked the insurance business from the consumer side my entire professional life. If I haven't seen it, heard it, said it, or done it, then it's only because I shredded it. These are things such as:

- If you hand a workers' compensation auditor a shoebox full of W-2s and a handwritten ledger sheet, he or she will find something in those files that will cost you a great deal of money, regardless of any other circumstance.

- If your boss tells you to subrogate, don't ask him what subrogation really means. It ticks bosses off because they don't really know what subrogation means, either.

- Never call up the owner's brother-in-law and ask him how drunk he was when he totaled the company car.

- There are some auto appraisers who steer their policyholders to certain repair facilities because these shops indulge the appraisers in their excesses, such as booze and women.

- If you have a totaled automobile, the insurance adjuster will write the appraisal for "visible damage only." In order to get the actual extent of the damage, he will ask you to tear the vehicle down. If the vehicle is non-repairable but not considered a total loss by the insurer, you lose all the value from the salvage because you tore the vehicle down.

What I offer here are opportunities for significant cost savings in insurance that are right there in your insurance policies. There is nothing magical about any of these techniques. This is a comprehensive guide to managing your insurance program that will yield your company significant financial rewards.

Remember, if you save money on insurance, that savings is not tied to any profit margin or any offset; it is an immediate, positive bottom-line result.

How This Book Will Save You Money

When you finish this book, you will be able to do the following:

- Know the difference between types of insurance and understand what these policies do and do not cover.

- Understand the difference between a self-insured retention program and a deductible program and how the structure of these programs can cost you big cash.

- Know the difference between admitted and non-admitted carriers and what that difference can mean to your organization.

- Explain what subrogation means.

- Understand the difference between a garage policy and a garage keepers' legal liability policy.

- Determine how bonds used as security for an insurance program can significantly affect your bottom line and how to avoid the adverse consequences.

- Tell the difference between underwriters and actuaries. (I'll give you a hint: the underwriter is someone the insured has never met; the actuary is someone no one has ever met.)

- Effectively manage your claims load.

This text can also be used as a reference guide to provide short-and long-term direction on targeted areas of concern, as in the following situations:

- You have an audit coming up, and you need to prepare.

- Your in-house counsel wants to litigate a liability claim.

- You are asked to determine the difference in cost between the current property coverage and the value of a blanket policy.

- You are wondering whether self-insurance is right for your company.

- What about captives?

- You need to know whether a delay in reporting a claim will adversely affect your premium.

- You want to know where you can find out whether your employees are covered when working in another state.

Similarly, the glossary is an invaluable tool when you need a quick explanation. For example, you might be in a meeting where someone says, "We are closing in on the anniversary of the '02 policy on the retro work comp policy. Since this policy is based on total incurred losses instead of paid losses, we will need to determine the percentage rebate only after the anniversary date actually occurs."

At that point, you can excuse yourself, run back to your office, and look up "retro" in the glossary, which explains that this is a retrospectively rated program. It also explains in simple terms the difference between a paid loss and an incurred loss program. By the way, there is a huge difference. Then, you can run back into the meeting and know what everyone is talking about. The glossary is a particularly valuable tool because it provides simple explanations of insurance terms.

The Insurance Guy

All the situations described in this chapter are mistakes that I have made. And there are more—many more. In the past twenty years, I have screwed up more situations than I care to admit. When I first started out, I had no idea of how the insurance industry worked, so most of my experiences have come from trial and error. And through it all, I have consistently lowered insurance costs for the company I worked for by an average of 1 to 3 percent of gross revenue!

Imagine the savings I could have realized if I had known what I was doing.

When I received the designation Associate in Risk Management (ARM) in 1996, it validated my knowledge of insurance within the business community. It was this educational experience that taught me the language, processes, and elements of insurance to effectively advise my company and manage their comprehensive insurance program. This was one of the hardest series of courses I had ever experienced, because it gave me the foundation upon which to grow.

By the time I received my CPCU designation, I found the courses much easier to navigate because of my almost twenty years experience as a risk manager. These courses helped to fill in the blanks in those areas of insurance that I had never been exposed to or that I had been exposed to but didn't really care about. Not only that, it also validated my experience to those within the insurance industry, although I have never worked in the insurance industry.

And that, ladies and gentlemen, is my strength.

My experience outside of the insurance industry allows me to convey this information without the encumbrances and biases of the insurance industry. My industry education validates my knowledge and certifies me as an insurance professional.

It's the best of both worlds. If you read this book, you won't have to hide from the insurance guy. There will be no need to.

Why People Hate Insurance

My daughter is now taking algebra. At some point, she is going to ask me why she has to learn this, since no one ever uses this stuff.

"Ah, but you're wrong, my dear," I will say. "Risk managers do."

Rick leaves his house and proceeds to work. There, he is told that his company has had an average of 290 accidents per year. Twenty-four of these involved an injury that required medical attention, 47 were injuries that only required first aid, and the rest were property damage. Using gross revenue of $12,450,000 as the benchmark, determine the percentage of accidents per category and compare those numbers to past years, tying the number to the amount of gross revenue in each applicable year.

Yes, that's algebra. I would invite anyone to come over and discuss this further.

Ultimately, you will have an opportunity to understand, in simple terms, how insurance works and, more to the point, how *your* insurance works. From there, you can make informed decisions about the future course of your insurance program, which can save you 1 to 3 percent or more a year in costs as a percentage of your gross revenue. Just think: if your company generates $20,000,000 per year in gross revenues, and you are able to knock just 1 percent off of your insurance costs, you will save $200,000 per year. That alone should be worth the price of this book.

2

Insurance, the Necessary Evil

Your First Brush with Business Insurance

Most small businesses start out the same way. You're working for someone else, sitting in a cubicle that the company calls your modular workspace. You sit and dream of the day you can tell the bosses to take a hike and finally go out on your own. Reality quickly sets in. You realize you have the wife, kids, and mortgage, and thoughts of running your own business quickly fade into the reality of the day.

Then something happens—a life-changing event. Your company of fifteen years suddenly becomes insolvent. You lose a parent or a loved one. You suddenly realize that the priorities of yesterday have faded somewhat. It's time to take a shot.

You inherit some money or meet up with someone who has the cash but not the time, and it provides the resources to go in a different direction.

So you start the process. You take time off from work with your vacation days to meet with potential investors. You meet with a banker, develop a business plan, and line up initial capital financing. You may even refinance the mortgage.

You sit with your wife, who will do the books until the business gets off the ground. The two of you mull over the pluses and minuses and decide to literally go for broke.

You have a couple of people who are interested in what you're selling. Your product and/or services just need to get out there. You learn all about incorporating—sub-S versus Limited Liability Company (LLC), partnerships—and you make a decision. You then get the papers drawn up. All you need now are the permits, and you're in business.

At this point, everything starts to fit together. People are interested, others are willing to bankroll you, and you begin to see the vision. Only a few weeks ago, it was a dream. Now, it's becoming a reality—a dream come true. So why do you still have that knot in your stomach that won't go away?

The reason is that the dream *is* a reality, and it's a little easier to solve complex business problems in your head than in the real world.

You go down to the county office to register the business, and everything is going swimmingly. Oh, the clerk has one more question, "Who is insuring this business?"

Your mind comes to a screeching halt. Insurance? Why do I need insurance? I thought I would get insurance when the company actually started to make some money.

"What are your limits?"

What are limits? At this point, you're hoping they haven't yet hired your replacement at your old job.

"How many employees do you have?" the clerk asks.

"Oh, just two: my wife and me."

"Good," replies the clerk. "In this state, as long as you have two employees or fewer, including yourself, workers' compensation is not required. If you add the third employee, though, the law requires you to have this coverage."

OK, fine. She says I don't need it, I don't need it.

You head over to the bank, and the bank's representative asks whether you are bonded. He also asks that the bank be named as additional insured. You try to nod knowingly, figuring that GL stands for general ledger and that your wife would handle that.

You run home, and your wife explains to you that you're an idiot and that GL stands for general liability—coverage that you have on your home but not on the business. She also says she thinks they call it CGL for commercial general liability.

Frantically, you call your brother-in-law, Bob, who, when sober, is your insurance agent. He thinks you say you want a CSL, so he increases your auto limits from 100/300/100 to a combined single limit of $500,000.

Huh?

"You gotta have it," says Bob. "Everybody has to have it. That's what I love about this business. It really never cuts into my happy hour—er, leisure time. But what does this have to do with the business?" he asks.

You finally explain to him what you need, and he is able to provide you with an umbrella policy that will drop down in some instances, and also adds some inhouse office coverage as well as some inventory coverage for the materials you have yet to buy.

You have no idea what you have just bought, and it sure was expensive, but you're covered now. You remember thinking that you hope the insurance is not as shaky as your brother-in-law.

He names the bank as additional insured for a fee, although they don't receive it for ten days because their insurance office is in Cleveland, and sending it to the branch means it's somewhere on Madge's desk.

Finally, you get the call that everything is in order, and you start your new business.

Starting to sound familiar? OK, then, let's continue.

The Business Gets Going

You're in business selling digital software that can provide a video feed, as well as regular photo prints, so that parents of newborns can monitor the baby twenty-four hours a day. You sell a few custom systems, but after eight months the business is not taking off.

To provide additional income, you use the business's structure to start cleaning houses. You and your wife clean while the kids are at school. The wife, though, is getting pretty tired of this.

Then you receive an offer to clean an office building, which would have to be done at night. You hire the kid down the street, who is home from college for the summer, as well as an applicant whom you found through an ad in the paper. You remember what you were told when you incorporated: any more than two employees and workers' compensation is required.

So you call your brother-in-law, but he doesn't do commercial insurance, so he refers you to a broker who is on his bowling team. You bring in your information, along with the copy of the contract from the property management office, and you get a price—an outrageous price in your estimation, but a price nonetheless.

You call around to see if you can get a better price, but since your business has no history, you are an "assigned risk," and you must pay the applicable surcharges. So what do you do?

OK, let's pause here for a moment.

For you folks who started your businesses from the ground up, I'm sure you can relate to some of this. The priority when you get started is attracting business, servicing accounts, and developing relationships. There isn't enough time to worry about the insurance coverage.

And let's face it. There really isn't that much to lose. With little or no equity in the business, if someone sues and the insurance isn't there, the other party isn't going to get much.

So why worry?

The Business Really Gets Going

So you pay what you consider an outrageous price for the coverage. In the meantime, you go to a barbecue at the neighbor's house and meet someone who works in a local hospital. She hears your idea about using your webcam to tape the birthing of babies. You install a test site in one birthing room, and the idea is so popular that the administration of the hospital contracts for you to provide this service at all its hospitals in the region.

At the same time, you now have four crews cleaning three high-rises, and you are moving into your own office space with a warehouse adjacent to the office.

Then the baby video thing starts to lose steam as digital cameras and video recorders become more popular. Look on the bright side: you could have invested in pay phones. Your investment in the project, as well as the cost of taking the equipment out, is about to financially sink the entire operation.

Then the property manager at the high-rises calls to schedule some janitorial service. He happens to mention that he has been ordered to put video surveillance cameras in each of the thirty-five office buildings he has recently started managing.

You bid the contract and get it. You then take the equipment from the hospitals, modify it for the security system, and install it in that building and four other buildings the company manages.

Life is good.

Why So Many Businesses Consider Insurance a Necessary Evil

The first "moment of truth" occurs in your business when you realize that this dream of yours might actually turn into something more than you'd ever imagined. You finally come to that day of reckoning when you actually believe in the business and your ability to succeed in business as an owner/operator.

In this case the decision to get workers' compensation insurance is an easy one; the property management company needs evidence that you have workers' compensation or the deal's off.

Often, though, a small business will be shortsighted and try to get away with not having insurance because they think it is so expensive that the business won't make any money.

This type of business usually runs its course and goes out of business within a year or two, since they begin to believe that they really don't need insurance to cover the loss exposures that can occur in the course of a business day. The problem lies in the fact that not only is the size of the business growing, which increases your risk, but also the organization has assets that need to be protected to support the infrastructure created through this growth.

Remember, in the beginning you didn't worry so much about the need for insurance to protect your assets, because you didn't have any assets to protect. Also, with a small operation, there is less chance for loss because of the size of the operation. The businesses that succeed beyond this initial moment of truth are those that realize that insurance coverage is an absolute necessity.

Unfortunately, it is so expensive that it leaves a bad taste in your mouth. You're also not sure whether your coverage will truly cover all the organization's risk, and the only person who can provide you with any of these answers is the guy who is selling you the insurance—*the broker*. And he just bought a new boat and he's invited you to go fishing!

So when the first few claims come down the pike, you may be inclined to wash your hands of it, sending them along to the insurance company with a note that says, in effect, "We pay you a lot of money; you handle it."

This frustration comes from expecting the expense to be tied to results. Try as you might, you just can't seem to see the overall value for the money you are paying. So far, insurance has depleted any profit you may have made, protecting assets that don't really exist, and generally just ticking you off.

There are some common and simple questions that most, if not all, new business owners ask when it comes to insurance. There are a multitude of reasons why many businesses do not try to understand insurance and the entire risk-management process.

Sure, it's based on contracts, but you look at contracts all the time. Insurance folks also speak another language, and most lay folks nod and pretend they understand, but, for the most part, it might as well be Greek.

But there is one overriding reason there is not a lot of emphasis on insurance, and it's pretty simple if you think about it. Insurance is really, really boring! Tedious, technical, complicated—boring!

Fascinating? Yes. We are always fascinated by that which we don't understand.

- How do they have enough money to pay for those hurricane losses?

- How do they figure out how much to charge me?

- I was always told that my auto rates would go down when I turned twenty-five, but when I did, my rates actually went up. What's up with that?

Intriguing? Again, yes. I mean, how do they determine that hail indeed hit my house, but it wasn't the hail from last week's storm, but rather the storm that hit two years and one day ago? And, of course, since I have two years to make a claim, it's not covered.

Confusing? I'll let you answer that. I picked the following wording out of a common insurance policy at random. "If a loss is partly recoverable under this policy and partly recoverable under a prior policy containing a deductible, the deductible amount specified in this policy shall be reduced by the deductible amount applied to such loss by the prior policy."

Huh?

Try this one: "To the extent any coverage may otherwise be available under this policy, or any of its endorsements, the provision of this exclusion shall supersede the same and exclude such coverage."

Now, you may be able to put these clauses into the context of the policy and actually understand what it says. This premise assumes two things:

1. You will actually read the policy.

2. You actually care.

I once worked at a service company whose sales department couldn't understand why their customers needed to have minimum limits of insurance. The funny thing is that they understood why the insurance was necessary; they just couldn't understand why *their* customers needed it. The problem was twofold: they didn't understand it, and they failed to include it as a requirement until after the agreement was made (and sometimes even after the contract was signed). If the sales department does not stipulate insurance coverage from the customer, the company selling the product or service needs to provide the coverage, without building the amount of the insurance cost into the price.

Heck, anyone can sell products and services if they give away the farm.

It got so bad that the company's executive committee asked me to report to them during their next weekly meeting so we could come to consensus. I love that word, "consensus"—from the Greek, meaning "Do what I tell you."

Well, I made copies of all the company's insurance policies and proceeded to review each policy with the executive committee, page by page, explaining why it was imperative that the insurance needed from customers should stay where it was.

This lasted about thirty-five minutes, which was approximately thirty minutes after I had lost the entire room. I then explained (in a not-so-subtle monotone) the history of how these limits came to be required, and I was out of there in less than an hour.

Each executive made a point of giving the paperwork back to me, and although there were rumblings from sales and marketing from time to time, I never had to explain this again.

Why?

Because their eyes glazed over, they decided they weren't going to figure it out in one day, and they deluded themselves into thinking they didn't need to understand this insurance stuff, which was good—since it is so boring! And, since they had me, and it appeared that I knew what I was talking about, they figured there was really no reason for anyone else to get involved in the process.

This is an actual quote from an executive in that organization that day:

"And *you* can't make me."

The Baffle Factor

The insurance people know this, and they use it to their advantage. Try this out the next time the opportunity arises. When you have your first contact with a member of the insurance industry, listen closely. They will use phrases that you think make them sound fairly knowledgeable and perhaps even intelligent. Phrases like "it is contingent upon" and "it all depends on your status as the additional insured." They will start to talk about probability versus possibility. At this point, you're thinking that they really know what they're talking about.

The word "underwriting" will generally come up within the first few minutes of that initial conversation. Are they trying to impress you? Are they trying to baffle you into a clear position of submission? Is this the way they talk at home?

Actually, what they are usually doing is gauging your knowledge of insurance and how it relates to your organization. They are testing you to see how much you know.

Most people are genuinely baffled by insurance. It really isn't an even playing field out there. Nobody wants to take the time to learn this stuff, yet it is imperative, if not mandatory, to learn all you can to maximize your company's value.

Some insurance industry folks have a tendency to turn their noses up at the rest of commerce. It's that sort of "I know all about this, and you don't, so don't ask any questions" mentality.

For example, I went to a new company and started asking the company's broker some questions. Knowing their attitude and approach, I played dumb and asked things like "What does contingency mean?" and "Can't you charge us a little less for this stuff?"

The responses came back, and they started to tell me that "This is how things are run around here" and "You won't be around here long if you don't fall in line."

This was from the broker! In the meantime, I would go to meetings with the broker and our executives, and my side would ask some very intelligent questions. This is more or less the way the last one went.

Executive: "Well, Mr. Broker, what do you think the solution to this exposure is?"

Mr. Broker: "Well, what do you think?"

Executive: "I think we should buy this coverage for this specific loss exposure from you for an outrageous amount, so that I can truly feel that we're covered, whether we are or not."

Mr. Broker: "Is that what you really think?"

Executive: "Yes, I do."

Mr. Broker: "Then that is what we should do. Do you have time for lunch?"

I felt like I was in group therapy instead of an insurance meeting. The last straw was this young kid who was working claims for the broker. He started lecturing me on the ins and outs of how insurance companies' claims departments work and why I should just send in the paperwork and get out of the way.

Gee, I wonder what those guys are doing these days.

This particular broker was the only broker this organization ever had, which would have been fine, except that they treated our account as what I like to call a "rollover." This means that they assumed we were going to renew with them since we never marketed the program to other brokers. These guys would come in midterm and tell the owners that the market was bleak and that costs could go up as high as 30 percent over last year. Then they would come back with an average increase between 10 and 15 percent at the eleventh hour, and they looked like heroes.

The broker made a good assumption for about ten years and then got greedy. They did a limited amount of work, knowing that the company had neither the time nor the inclination to move the program. By the time the program was shopped, they had oversold the account to the point of no return.

When the competition came back with significant price breaks and much more attractive financial security requirements, the incumbent broker's attempt to match these numbers toed the line between silliness and outright deception. It was difficult to watch.

It's All about the Cash

This kind of understanding will help any business save a significant amount of money in their insurance program. And this is the stuff that money is made of. I know you want to learn this stuff, but the boring factor and the learning curve make it almost impossible.

Well, I cannot completely overcome the dullness of the subject matter, but I am going to simplify things so you know where to look, what to do, and which questions you need to ask. This is twenty years of knowledge, education, and experience from a business perspective, all wrapped up in a tight little package. And maybe I'll get to poke some fun at the industry and at myself as we go.

Insurance made simple—this is the first book that gives you all this information, from the eyes of the businessperson, in a simple and easy format. If you are ready to make your insurance program as cost-effective as possible and generate some real savings, this is where the information is.

Let's start by answering some of the pressing questions most people have when it comes to insurance.

Frequently Asked Questions

Do you pay more for insurance when you start a business than when your business takes off?

Of course you do, and here's why. When you turn eighteen, you walk into a new car dealership, pick out a nice shiny new car, and are turned down flat for financing. Why? You have no credit history, no baseline from which the lender can determine your creditworthiness.

Five years later, the same dealership will sell you a car with some money down with a reasonably good, but not great, interest rate.

Twenty years later, you walk in, pick out a vehicle, and sign the paperwork with no cash down and zero percent financing. Why? Because the lender can see that you have a history of paying your bills, and you're a good credit risk.

It's the same with commercial insurance. There is a direct correlation between the type of claims history you have and the rate you pay.

The number of claims that you have (frequency) and the amount of money paid for claims (severity) have a direct impact on the amount you pay for insurance. And there are simple strategies to lessen the frequency and severity of losses, which I will cover in later chapters.

Once you have established your organization with a better-than-average loss history, you begin to find interest from brokers who want that kind of business. Everyone wants your business, but just as a new manager needs to be the right fit, your broker must be a good fit as well.

He or she must be knowledgeable about the industry, yet still inquisitive. You need to find a broker who can take your strengths and sell them to the insurance companies, while providing you with future strategies for improvement. This will lead to a reduction in losses, which in turn will make your account more attractive to the marketplace and more valuable to the broker.

What If I Don't Understand Insurance?

The first step is to get away from the idea that insurance is evil. If you truly believe this, then you are accepting the high cost of insurance as a given, and until you change your mindset, your insurance costs will continue to escalate. Insurance is a tool, and the management of this tool will help shape your organization's ultimate value.

Yes, I did say value. Just as you hire professionals to run your key departments, you need to look at your insurance program as a process that must be managed to produce effective results.

From the initial premium deposit throughout the entire claims process, it is imperative that your company have someone in the organization who is knowledgeable enough to manage the process from start to finish.

This doesn't have to be a full-time employee, if you feel you can't commit the resources to the establishment of an insurance and risk-management department. It can be a payroll or human resources person. In any case, I would make sure that this manager gets some training, and then the rest they can learn in the pages of this book.

It can also be a risk-management consultant who can evaluate your program and assist you with its administration. I know—a lot of you are saying at this point that you don't even know where your policies are, much less how to organize the program. Your company may be a good candidate for hiring a consultant to organize and evaluate your program.

A good risk-management consultant can generally identify deficiencies in your coverage. A great risk manager will be able to identify which coverage is generally not necessary—things that are in place only to serve the good fortune of your broker, rather than actually insuring a real loss exposure.

The next step is to understand that risk management is a discipline. It has its own standards, its own rules, and its own language. Have you ever had a conversation with a broker who told you that after a thorough analysis of your organization, he or she has narrowed your needs to a retro plan or a deductible, although the retro would involve a commitment to safety in the future, while a deductible plan would be a little more expensive due to a spotty recent claims history? Both plans would probably cost more money unless you do something about reducing your frequency of claims, which tends to turn into "the hard market is going to turn," blah blah blah, "the hurricanes caused the market to," blah blah blah, and on, and on, and on.

They begin to sound like the adults on a *Peanuts* special. You begin to lose interest, and before you know it, you decide on the same old first-dollar, guaranteed cost program with a 10 to 15 percent increase.

Why? Because you can't understand the plan? No!

Tell me how much it costs and when the bill is due. My ears are bleeding! Here's your check, now LEAVE ME ALONE!

This is where you need to change.

Do I really need to read all the insurance policies?

Yes, you do. I know, I know. You would rather stick a needle in your left eye than read an insurance contract. Someone within your organization needs to make sure that these policies cover what the broker agreed to.

Insurance policies are not just legal contracts; they are also "contracts of adhesion," which means that one party (the insurance company) writes the contract and the other party (you) must accept or reject the contract as written.

Knowing this gives you a distinct advantage when a claim occurs. If the insurance language is ambiguous and confusing, the courts will side with the party who signed the contract, since the writer of the contract has a duty to use clear language to avoid such confusion.

A few years back, a member of my immediate family became ill. Now, don't get me wrong, I have found most health insurance companies to be very helpful—*until someone gets sick.* Then they started to deny claims for things I understood to be covered. Now, the insurance policy (evidence of coverage) is sixty-three pages long, plus endorsements, which make changes to the first sixty-three pages.

That's a lot of *wherefores* and *neverminds,* but I began to read it with my one good eye. On more than one occasion, I actually fell asleep looking at the policy on the computer screen. The stuff is really droll, and in my opinion, it is intended to be that way.

Well, I found the answer on page forty-one, with no amending of the policy to preclude it. I appealed to the carrier and to the broker. Within twenty-four hours, I received a call from my human resources department, saying it was not covered since the company had not agreed to that.

But…but…but…that's not what it says. The HR gal shot back that they wrote it, but we didn't pay for it, it wasn't covered, and the insurer must have made a mistake.

Remember, if you can find it in your policy, and you understand the intent of what the language is providing, you will be covered. Of course, the opposite is true as well. If the insurance company does not put in the language to cover the loss, they will not cover it.

Eventually the insurer did pay the claim, and immediately changed the language.

There are two ways to avoid this and make sure you're covered:

1. Read the policies.

2. Have the broker draft a letter of understanding at the commencement of the policy period, which spells out what coverage was agreed to, as well as the terms of the financing.

Why? In some instances, it may take up to six months to get the policies from the insurance carrier. In the meantime, this letter of understanding will clear up any ambiguities and could be the difference between a loss being covered or denied.

Read the policies. You never know what you might learn.

> *Is my insurance program the one that is best for my organization, or is it just a cash cow for the broker and the insurance company?*

In college, I had a job waiting tables in an Italian restaurant. The first thing the owner told me was, "If you're asked what's good on the menu, tell them the veal."

"Oh," I said, "the veal is good here?"

"No, you idiot, it's the most expensive thing on the menu."

When I sold cars, I made a little on the sale of the vehicle, but I made a lot if I was able to get customers to finance through the dealership, buy the undercoating, upgrade the stereo, or purchase a maintenance program. My job was to convince them that they needed what I had to sell.

Telling buyers that my kids' next meal depended on them taking the extended service plan made me look kind of desperate. (I only tried it once—OK, twice.)

Brokers make good money selling you basic insurance coverage. They make great money if they sell you extra stuff that you may or may not need. The only way to determine if you need it is to know what they're selling.

Once you, as a businessperson, understand that insurance is a business tool that can be used to your advantage, you can begin to develop a philosophy to which insurance costs can be reduced, mitigated, and quantified well into the future.

Insurance does not have to be a mystery, although your lack of knowledge gives the industry a distinct advantage.

> *Do I really need to get all the coverage my clients ask for in their contracts? (e.g., if I contract to do a job, and they need evidence of insurance I don't have, do I need to go and get it?)*

Yes and no. You can negotiate with customers to lower the requirements, but it is usually best for building goodwill if you don't do this, especially with the amount of insurance you have (coverage limits).

In fact, if you call a business and ask the certificate person why they need the limits of insurance they ask for, more often than not he or she will tell you that this is what it says on the checklist. You could proceed up the ladder, but you will find very few people who know why the limits and language requirements are what they are. If you proceed to the executive level and they are unable to explain why and are unwilling to reduce the limits (which would contradict the checklist), your company may develop a reputation as being difficult to deal with, and this could impact your ongoing relationships.

On the other hand, the customer may ask your organization to insure them for anything that occurs for the duration of the contract. In that case, you can usually cross out this language, which is generally not enforceable, and the client uses it only as a point of negotiation. You give us this, and we'll amend that.

More often than not, though, no one really knows why the limits are set or why the wording on the certificate must be just so. Nobody knows, nobody really wants to know, and nobody cares.

Why, you ask? Because it's insurance, by golly!

Remember, though, that anything you agree to by contract usually kicks in only if there has been negligence on your part. For example, I once came upon a general liability "slip and fall" incident in which it was alleged that a pedestrian injured himself when he slipped on some materials left by our worker. Although we were not named in the suit, our general liability believed that our organization had a duty to defend the property owner, although no negligence on our part could be proved.

I quizzed the insurance company, and they verified that they had a duty to defend but not to indemnify, meaning we had to hire and pay the lawyers, but we didn't have to pay the claim.

I called the insurance adjuster for the property owners, and asked them to accept the defense on this. When they refused, I asked our adjuster to find out how much the claimant wanted, and to settle for that amount, sending the bill to the other carrier.

The other carrier accepted responsibility to defend their own case almost immediately. They didn't want me playing with their money.

The bottom line is if you can buy it, do it. The amount of goodwill with your clientele is well worth the cost. And it limits your interface with the sales department, which is always just fine with me, since they are usually mad at me about something.

Read on. Help is here.

Will you know everything about insurance upon completion of this text?

Absolutely not. No one person knows everything there is to know about insurance, but you will have enough of an understanding of the insurance process to ask intelligent questions, make informed decisions, and reduce costs by purchasing coverage that is in the best interest of your organization's bottom line—not the bottom line of your broker or of some unknown underwriting department.

Underwriters give the brokers pricing options, and the broker determines which policy would be best for them to sell you. But is it the best for you?

And seriously, has anyone ever met an underwriter?

Are you going to tell me to go to seminars and insurance conferences to increase my knowledge of the insurance industry?

In one of the Winnie-the-Pooh movies, there was a character—a gopher, I think—who was kind of a repair guy. When Pooh (a bear of very little brain) asked him where he could reach him, he would respond "not in the book." This meant not only that he was not in the phone book, but also that he was a character made up just for the movie. You will not find him in any of the Winnie-the-Pooh books.

Until now, this information was not in the book.

Just read the book.

It's All in the Book

3

What the Heck Is Risk Management?

I have been in the risk-management arena since 1988. In 1988, risk management was not much of an arena; it was more of a club.

In fact, it was more like a junior high school gym where the bleachers fold out for special activities. Although there were plenty of us around back then, most of us just didn't admit to being risk managers, and certainly very few got together to hang out. It's not so much that I was ashamed to be a risk manager. I just became uncomfortable with the inevitable follow up question: "So, what exactly does a risk manager do?"

Since 2001, though, more companies have seen the need to dedicate their resources to the management of insurance and risk. The stark reality of the 9/11 attacks made a lot of businesspeople wake up to the realization that until they start managing their risk and insurance as well as they do the other aspects of their business, one incident, however isolated, could close the operation altogether.

The Evolution of Risk Management

This is how I saw risk management evolve in the 1980s through the 1990s. A small company would have a bookkeeper that would evolve into an accounting department. Insurance would be handled by the owner or his main executive, and the day-to-day activities concerning insurance would be handled by accounting, since they paid the bills.

Accounting would also handle any audits for policies that require it, and claims would be sent from the field directly to the broker, who would file it with the carrier. Insurance was something you had to have, and the only thing accounting knew about it was that the bill had to be paid, on time, or bad things would happen.

In fact, most companies learn about the ramifications of not paying insurance bills on time the first time they decide to pay something else. ("What are they gonna do, cancel our insurance?")

In the 1990s came a whole bunch of regulatory stuff that made it necessary for companies to dedicate funds to human resources to ensure that I-9s, employee benefits, COBRA, and later HIPPA were being managed effectively. Human resources would be separate from payroll, and to help round out the day, HR would also handle claims and insurance.

Why? Because both involved a great deal of paperwork, so if you could find someone who was good at HR paperwork, they would probably be good at insurance paperwork. This usually becomes necessary because after a human resources department is formed, accounting doesn't want to do insurance anymore.

Again you ask why. Because it's boring! It's pretty sad when an accountant tells you what you do is boring. My boss recently cancelled a meeting, saying something about how he'd rather watch grass grow, or some such thing. Once I had an executive cancel an insurance meeting to watch training videos—in Spanish! The point is that most companies would know more about insurance products and services if it didn't cause their brains to hemorrhage.

As these companies continued to grow, as most companies did during the Internet explosion in the mid to late 1990s, they would branch out the insurance function to a dedicated department.

They called this department risk management, basically, because it sounded cool. Unfortunately, when the IT bubble burst and companies needed to downsize, risk management would be one of the first casualties and would be shuffled back to HR. Last in, first out. Last department formed, first department dissolved.

At that point, though, the program usually had become a little too sophisticated to handle, so most organizations would lean more on their brokers who expanded their services to meet their clients' needs.

This reliance on brokers came with the management premise that it was more cost-effective to farm out various functions to other companies (outsourcing). On the insurance end of the business, it was only natural to farm this business out to your broker, who had the skills, expertise, and staff to accommodate your organization's needs.

Is this an effective way to manage your insurance needs? Would you ask your car salesman to manage your fleet? Would you ask an office supply sales rep to stock all your offices for you? It's not a question of whether or not you can trust these people. You can't.

And it's not their fault. It's just that your business is not their business. And their loyalty ultimately lies elsewhere.

Then comes 9/11, and everything changes. Although the overall impact of the event is widely understood and accepted, it is my opinion that the insurance industry used this catastrophic event to turn a soft market artificially hard. It raised prices significantly, while taking the opportunity to divest itself of risks it had been forced to take because of a soft market which had lasted almost twice as long as anticipated.

The industry will argue that this was merely a correction. I feel the insurance industry took this opportunity, which they had not had in a long time, to raise prices that had been market driven for so long. Once things calmed down a little, the market brought prices back down to tolerable levels.

Then there is the terrorism coverage thing. The federal government mandated terrorism coverage and agreed to back it up, since no insurers would write it on the heels of 9/11. This is actually a good thing. Terrorism coverage is a good thing. Of course, being fewer than two miles from the Pentagon and the White House makes me a little more fearful than most.

The best thing about this from a risk-management standpoint is that there has not been one terrorist attack on American soil since the 9/11 attacks. So you have this entire terrorism premium, hundreds upon millions of dollars, and you look at the loss history: *Number of Claims—0; Total Amount Paid Nationwide—0.*

An industry can get pretty healthy pretty quick with that kind of return. The best part is if the government allows this law to expire (sunset), the industry will stop providing the coverage, since it cannot "afford" the losses without government backing. The insurers would then walk away with all that premium.

Of course, with an election looming in 2006, Congress decided to extend the terrorism coverage for two years, each year exposing the industry to more risk and responsibility.

What does that mean for you and me? Higher rates, of course.

I know what you're thinking here—you're in the wrong business. Well, it's really not as easy as it looks. Insurance is a necessity and not because of 9/11. It's always been a necessity. Most organizations would be unable to get out of the gate without taking some risks, and insurance provides a buffer against these risks.

Now, I am going to tell you something here that may shock you.

The insurance industry has lots and lots of money!

This money is generated from premiums which in turn are reinvested to generate more cash. There are limits on where and how much can be invested, but the bottom line is—*the insurance industry as a whole has a really good bottom line!*

I have seen statistics that show that most insurance companies lose money on their claims handling, but these losses are more than offset by investment returns.

This is also not a bad thing. The problem lies in the marketing of insurance products. Some underwriters and brokers take advantage of the ignorance of the business community to create an opportunity to sell more than the business client may actually need. Most companies will over indemnify because they don't want to look pound foolish should they make a wrong decision to save some pennies.

The insurance industry will have you believe that the reason claims costs are so high is because of the extreme service and benefits provided. There is some value to this argument, but unfortunately it holds very little weight. In fact, the real culprits are market conditions and the industry's inability and/or unwillingness to adapt.

The Gramm-Leach-Bliley Act (1999)

The rules changed in 1999 with a federal law that was long in coming. Signed into law in 1999 as the Financial Services Modernization Act, it is more commonly known as the Gramm-Leach-Bliley Act, which now allows banks to offer insurance products and insurance companies to offer banking services (both through holding companies).

The increased competition, along with both industries tapping into their client base to raid customers from the other industry, has provided for market-driven price reductions and a lower standard for underwriting to remain competitive in the marketplace.

This provides opportunities for value and savings in insurance at all levels.

The Risk-Management Process

So what is risk management?

If you look it up, you will find that risk management is a process, and the process involves six steps:

1. Identify your loss exposures (a loss is when something happens; a loss exposure is something that could happen).

2. Analyze those loss exposures you identified (loss prevention—is there any way I can change the way I do things to prevent these exposures and their eventual losses? Loss reduction—is there anything I can do to minimize losses I cannot prevent?).

3. Examine alternatives—should I just continue with the same guaranteed cost coverage/first-dollar coverage or should I look at a more creative program which may include deductibles, SIRs, retros, or maybe even a captive?

4. Select the program.

5. Implement it.

6. Monitor it to make sure it's working and adapt as necessary.

The ABCs of the Risk-Management Process

Let's simplify this even more. Take out a piece of paper and a pencil. Draw a square to represent the largest facility you have. Then start answering these questions:

1. Do you own the facility? If yes, is the replacement amount on the policy sufficient to cover a total loss to that facility? If no, do you have the proper coverage as required by the lease?

2. Are customers regularly on the premises? If yes, does my present coverage adequately protect me from them?

3. Are there employees on the premises? How many? Who does what? (Draw in stick people if you like—this is the creative portion of the program.)

4. Is there inventory on premises? Is it properly valued to cover a loss? (Draw small boxes within larger box.)

5. Is there equipment on-site which is leased and, if owned, properly valued? (Use your imagination.)

6. Would the loss of a piece of equipment interrupt the entire process? If the answer is yes, would this disruption cause a significant loss to the organization? Is the company covered under any of the present coverage?

7. Do you depend on suppliers for key aspects of this process, and if so, would the loss of this supplier interrupt the process in any way?

8. Are there vehicles at this facility? Personal passenger vehicles, light trucks, delivery vehicles, big rigs?

9. Is there a security system for the buildings as well as grounds/parking areas?

10. Is there a computer system on the premises? If so, is it part of a network or is the mainframe on-site?

11. Are there any environmental by-products which could be damaging if they escaped?

Now, draw another square a little lower to the right—lower, lower, right there. That's good. Now repeat the process for every facility you own/lease. You can start to draw lines between the facilities, asking more questions:

1. Do I have inventory that fluctuates between warehouses, and do those fluctuations need to be documented? Is the inventory covered, and will a loss cause a financial hardship to the organization?

2. If a vehicle travels into another state, or workers set up a jobsite in a specific state, are they covered? Remember, insurance is regulated by the states, so don't assume that the coverage in your jurisdiction is adequate when traveling to another jurisdiction.

3. If my sales managers fly to another location and rent a car, are they covered or do they need to get coverage through the car rental company?

Now, look at your diagram. Two squares, a few smaller squares, and some stickmen, and you have done a risk-management evaluation.

Don't look now, but you have answered a few very important questions.

Action Plan

OK, you have this information. Now what?

Remember, all these exposures are insurable. There are insurance companies out there who will insure anything. Energy companies insure against the weather; Bob Dylan insures his voice. After that one, no further example is needed.

If there is a financial consequence to a loss, you can find someone to indemnify it.

The question is price. Does it make good sense to insure losses that can easily be handled (retained) during the normal course of business as a current expense?

The rule of thumb here is called the law of large numbers, which means the more statistical information you have, the better you are able to predict how things will turn out in the future. So, if you have a bunch of small claims, over time you will begin to see trends developing which will enable you to predict with great accuracy the amount of claims you will have and the cost associated with these loss exposures.

If you track these little out-of-pocket losses, you will again begin to develop trends that will allow you to predict with a great degree of accuracy how much these small losses will cost you overall. If these numbers are higher than the cost to insure, then opt for insurance. If they cost less to handle in house, do that.

The book says you should retain losses that have high frequency and low severity. Conversely, you should insure losses with low frequency and high severity.

Let me explain this in the most technical terms I know: Pay the little losses that happen all the time and insure those big losses that don't happen so much.

Really big losses that could happen are not easy to predict, since they do not happen with a great degree of regularity, and the size of the loss could place the organization's future at risk.

Within the last three years, I got some pricing from a broker on some coverage. I questioned the cost, explaining that the organization had not had a loss that the insurance carrier had to pay in the last four years.

"You're due," she replied.

I hear she's now selling cars.

Statistically, she could justify this statement. Unfortunately, most of these statistics don't have much credence when it comes to your organization. It's like being told that if you buy a lottery ticket, and the chances of winning the big prize are a million to one, then buying two tickets reduces the odds to five hundred thousand to one. It just doesn't work that way.

Also, brokers spend all their time telling you that improving your loss history will help reduce your costs. Then, four or five years go by, and they try to increase your rates by predicting your future.

Far be it for me to say, but if they tell you that, you might have the wrong broker.

There are small losses that are insurable and that you may currently be insuring that your organization may decide to cover outside of insurance so as to keep claims activity to a minimum.

For example, a driver in a company vehicle hits a parked car, taking off a side-view mirror. In this instance, you could reimburse the other party (claimant) for the mirror. You would still have the choice of getting reimbursed from the carrier, but keeping the insurance company's costs down will only enhance your position when you renew the coverage.

The same goes for an employee injury which results in first-aid treatment. Workers' compensation in almost every state is governed by the rules of the National Council on Compensation Insurance, Inc. (NCCI), which rates your organization based on your frequency and severity of losses as reported by your work comp company.

A company with no history begins with an experience modification rate (mod rate) of 1.00. Based on the claims history, balanced with the amount of payroll, your company will be surcharged or receive a credit based on the loss history. A mod rate greater than one will result in a surcharge, while a mod rate of less than one will generate a credit.

This will be covered in more depth in a later chapter, but it is important to remember that your mod rate calculation values the number of claims (frequency) more highly than the amount (severity) of claims, which are generally capped.

I do want to emphasize that in the area of workers' compensation I always advocate acting in the best interest of the employee. In fact, in some states, you as the employer are actually required to report all work-related injuries to your comp carrier.

Find out what your state's requirements are instead of leaning on your broker for this information. Each state has a workers' compensation Web site that can give you this information. In fact, most of the questions you have can be found on these Web sites in their FAQ page.

Remember, mitigating losses enhances your position to reduce expense and enhance your bottom line.

It's that simple.

Am I a Risk Manager Yet?

Not yet, but you are well on your way.

By the way, the one good thing about being in risk management is that no one wants your job. Since insurance is so scary to most people, they really don't want to deal with the issues that come up on a daily basis.

Folks come to me all the time:

"Hey, whatcha doin'?"

"Nothing."

"Man, you guys in risk really have it made."

My reply is usually something like, "Really? Would you like to switch for a day or two?"

"What are you, nuts? I hate that stuff!"

Now I hear that kids are going to college to become risk managers. In 1986, it just didn't seem possible.

Wait, those kids may actually want my job.

Bummer.

4
Brokers

Friends, Compatriots, or Über-Salespeople

I had a dream last night. I dreamed that I needed to purchase a car to get back and forth to work. I walked into a dealership that sold economy as well as luxury vehicles. I told the salesman that I needed an inexpensive commuter car with good gas mileage, power windows and door locks, and a CD player. I walked out.

The salesman called about a week later and said he had my vehicle. I went back in, and he pulled up a brand-new Hummer with all the bells and whistles and a combined gas mileage rating of four miles per gallon.

I was puzzled.

"I just need a small car with good gas..."

"No, no, no! We are the experts here," said the salesman. "We have evaluated your needs and determined that this vehicle is the only vehicle that fits your needs and requirements. Did I mention that it gets four miles to the gallon?"

"OK, OK...what is this thing gonna cost me?" (It was very shiny—and red).

"Well, with taxes, tags, and all that, it comes out to about $57,500. But we also determined that you need to take the full extended warranty as well as the maintenance program, and the undercoating, which was already done at the factory especially for you. Total out the door $64,355. And since you have to be to work this afternoon, you are kind of out of options."

"And you're sure I need all this?"

"Yup."

"Well, I think I'll look around and see if I can get another offer."

"You can't do that," said the salesman. "When you came in here, you became mine, mine, mine, and you cannot go out and get prices from other dealers because the guys who do the pricing will get really mad at you.

"What if you go to our dealership in Podunk and they quote you a lower price. Those prices all come from the same source, and if that source finds out

38

they quoted two different prices to the same customer, they will get really mad at you…not me, *you*! And then this deal will be off the table. Seriously, this is how it works."

So I drove out in my overpriced Hummer, stopping to refill the tank before I got home. I had spent $50,000 more than I thought I would need to and because I talked to this guy first, I couldn't get a better deal elsewhere.

It also cost me quite a bit more on gasoline, although I did finance the maintenance up front. Hey, the guy said he knew what I needed, and he *is* the expert. Then I woke up. I was so relieved to realize that it was a dream and could never happen to anyone anywhere in the real world.

Don't be so sure!

How Did Your Last Insurance Renewal Go?

Let's see. Does your broker call you up about four months prior to the renewal and ask for a bunch of information so he or she can get you the best deal in the market? Do you send over the information as quickly as you can gather it and then quiz the broker on how he thinks it will go this year?

Does he tell you that the market is tight (hard market) or that the market is showing signs of softening up? Does he mention that there could be some savings next year, but that insurance rates have been going up in some cases 25 or 30 percent?

That's exactly what he told you last year. The market has hardened, is hardening, is showing signs of softening, and these price increases are out of anyone's control. He does say that this year, though, he will insist that the pricing folks (underwriters) not wait until the last day before the renewal date to get the prices over to you—another thing he said last year. All this and they've had four months to ponder the information.

So, fast forward four months—it's noon, the policy expires in twelve hours and one minute, and you still don't know what your numbers are going to be. Finally, all the numbers come in, and the increases are *only* between 15 and 20 percent. You're relieved because the broker had told you that premiums were increasing at a rate of 25–30 percent, so you got a deal. And, hey, when that market finally softens up, that will be the day your insurance ship comes in.

Sound familiar?

OK, let's say you get sick and tired of not having any options and decide to let other brokers come in and bid for the business with your current broker (broker of record) just to see what's out there.

Your guy calls you back and begins to explain that it's not good to shop the program, but if you insist on doing this, you need to make sure that no one goes to the same insurers or underwriter (assigning markets).

"Why?" you ask.

"Well, underwriters get really mad if they quote a price to one broker and another price to another broker, and if this happens the underwriter will get really mad at you and that may influence the price he gives you.

"The underwriter only wants to work with one broker per account."

You reply, "Isn't it your responsibility to know where your competitors go?"

"Well, yes, but with the insurance market not expected to soften up until next year at the very earliest, you could really hurt your chances."

Chances of what? You are expecting to pay premiums in excess of one million dollars this year, half of which is going to the policy written by this underwriter guy, whom you have never met. Is this company willing to walk away from this type of premium because they have to write two e-mails instead of one? Is that what they're telling you?

So, you do one of two things. You tell them that you will assign markets, but since you really don't know how to assign markets, you don't do it. Or you tell all the brokers who are quoting the program that you won't assign markets, but you will tell them who is competing for your business and it's up to them to decide where their competitors might go to place this insurance, and then they make their decisions accordingly.

Either way, about a month later, you will get a call from your current broker raising holy heck because one of the other brokers went to the same underwriting department at the same company, and the insurer is upset because one of the quotes was 10 percent less than the other.

Your reply, "I hope the lower quote is yours."

And, of course, this conversation is occurring two months before the renewal, and you can't understand why the quotes start coming in to you on the day before the renewal if the agents are getting competitive quotes two months before renewal.

"Listen, with your loss history, we can't afford to tick off this underwriting department," says the broker.

"Especially in a hard market that is showing signs of weakening, but not until next year," you interject.

"Yea, yea, that too."

So you agree at this point to assign the markets, and your current broker submits the names of insurers that he wants exclusive access to. When it comes across, you're relieved to see that it's only two pages. No, wait. That's just the "A's."

When you do this, you basically end up giving an exclusive to the current broker, and the rest of the competitors are left with crumbs—lower-rated companies, regional insurers, and non-admitted carriers. You end up renewing with the same tired old companies with a 15 to 20 percent increase in premium, which is significantly below the industry average increase of between 25 and 30 percent.

Or so they tell you.

If you assign markets to specific brokers, it pretty much defeats the purpose of shopping in the first place. The reason to shop is to determine if you are getting the best price in the market. I am not particularly concerned about whether or not the underwriters get their feelings hurt or the brokers get yelled at by the underwriters. Heck, it's not their fault; it's my fault.

But…if your account is valuable enough that the same underwriting company reviews it and agrees to quote it twice, you've got to figure that there is some other "A+" company out there willing to give that same number or something close to it.

How does an underwriter explain to his boss that they are walking away from five hundred thousand dollars in premium from a customer with a very good to excellent claims history that has generated a good profit for the insurance company?

"Well, they ticked me off because they wouldn't assign markets to the brokers, and because I'm an idiot and I don't know what's going on in my department, I quoted two different rates to two different brokers." Of course not, but that's what we're told year in and year out.

And it all happened because you did the following:

1. That's what the salesman told you that you need, and he's the expert.

2. According to the salesman, people get mad if you go anywhere else, and,

3. You are out of time, and you're happy to get something in place.

Keep All Your Marbles in One Sack

This is one quick but very important note: It is always best to keep all of your insurance with one broker, although you may change brokers from time to time. The reason is simple—administration. If you have half of your coverage with one broker and half with another, you will need to provide information to two sources when you need certificates for evidence of coverage.

And have you ever gotten a call from the foreman on the job or an administrator in the field who is not allowed to work because your certificate shows you don't have adequate coverage? You then would need to explain that your insurance business is with two different brokers and they are only looking at one of the certificates. To the person on the other end requesting such documents, it sounds just a little too confusing and perhaps a little bit shady.

Another issue that arises is when a customer needs specific wording on the certificate for general liability coverage. If two certificates come in, only one will have that specific wording, and you may find out you're experiencing delays because of this confusion, which is absolutely unnecessary.

Brokers generally see this as an advantage, but I see it as an opportunity. Since all brokers are aware that if they are successful in getting your account, they will get the entire program, it tends to make them very hungry and very aggressive in their pursuit of the deal, which gives you the opportunity for the best price in the insurance market. Some brokers will also cut their prices to the bone in the first year in the hopes of getting it all back sometime in the future.

The solution is to market the account every two to three years, even if you are completely satisfied with the performance of your current broker. Let each broker approach any market they please. I advocate this because it is the one way to ensure that you will get market prices for your program. If the broker is aware that you have no idea what the market will bear, and they have no competition, you're not going to get the best price. Period.

Not Just Any Broker

There are two broad considerations in selecting a broker. One, of course, is the price each brings to the table. The second, and equally important, aspect is their ability to service your account.

Does your broker understand the business you're in? Will he be able to service the volume of administrative requests and be responsive to field staff and customers?

Should you use a small broker or a conglomerate? This is a good question. Some companies like to be associated with a big regional or national brokerage network. Some companies believe they need a bigger broker to accommodate their needs, while others prefer a local broker who has a handle on the pulse of a centralized local economy.

With digital communication, there is really no need to have a local branch available to support your needs. Conversely, there is no reason to use a national firm when a local or regional group is suitable for your needs. It's like paying for Advil when ibuprofen does the job just as well. You are paying extra for the name.

I prefer using a midsized broker who is experienced in the industry and can handle the administration and customer service needs of my organization.

In a smaller brokerage firm, your account has more value to their business than one of those cookie-cutter brokerage firms. Smaller firms are generally more attentive to your needs because losing your account would have a greater impact on their bottom line.

In short, I find it's in my company's best interest to be a bigger fish in the smaller broker pond than a small fish in a conglomerate broker's pond.

If you go for price only, and the broker cannot produce the service necessary to accommodate your account, you stand to lose customer goodwill which will eventually fall to your bottom line.

The Broker Relationship

Remember when you first start the business and your drunken brother-in-law gets you coverage by putting endorsements on you personal policies? At some point, as the business grows, you determine that not only do you not want to involve your personal insurance in the business, but also that your company has outgrown your brother-in-law. So, you go out and find a commercial insurance broker, one who specializes in your type of business and comes highly recommended.

The commercial broker comes in, and in the first year saves you a whole bunch of money. You think that this guy or gal is the moon, the stars, and the sun when it comes to insurance. He takes you out to nice restaurants and sends you expensive wine and cheese baskets at Christmas. He tells you that although you are a client, he likes you and considers you a friend as well as a customer.

So why did he save you so much money? Is it because he is a "commercial insurance expert"? Possibly. Is he in tune with the insurance market that caters to your particular industry? Perhaps. Is it because your brother-in-law was so overwhelmed by a book of business to which he had no expertise, but you were the most lucrative account that he had? Exactly.

When a small company makes the transition to a broker who can market its business to the commercial insurance industry instead of using the most convenient resource available, the broker will save the company quite a bit of cash simply through his access to the commercial markets.

Also, if you started the relationship with the initial agent/broker because there was a personal relationship prior to the business relationship, it is not uncommon for you to wait a little longer to terminate the business relationship, especially if you are going to be sitting across from this person at Thanksgiving dinner.

When the transition does occur, however, the savings are generally immediate and substantial. So the broker comes in looking like a hero. Due to his initial performance, he has earned your trust. Each year, you renew at small increases, but for the first two or three years, it is not even close to approaching the premium you paid with your brother-in-law.

Hey, these folks are geniuses!

At some point, though, the current broker begins to realize that you are comfortable with him, and your company's account is not going anywhere. So he concentrates on new accounts as well as existing problem accounts.

In his mind, your account is a done deal (rollover account). Now, you may grumble and complain from time to time about the price. You may even tell them you are going to look for quotes elsewhere. If you do the latter, the broker will come over, climb up into your lap, give you a big hug, and tell you to trust him because he has never let you down before.

And since you really have no idea how to solicit business from another broker, and the current broker is "good folks," you stick around, suffering 15–20 percent increases each year for coverage you're not sure you need and you're not sure is adequate to cover all the loss exposures you have.

This is not how it has to be.

When Things Get Rough, Go Shopping

I shop for most of my business clothes at a rather expensive national clothing retailer. I cannot really justify the prices they are asking for suits, dress shirts, or ties. In fact, I am known as a pretty frugal (meaning cheap) guy.

Well, it just so happens that I have an outlet mall about ten miles from my home and this retailer has a shop in this outlet mall. I stop in there at least once a month. Sometimes I find sixty dollar shirts for five or ten dollars. One day, I stopped in, and they had suits marked down 50 percent in combination with a "buy one, get one free" deal. I walked out with three suits that retail for a total of about two thousand dollars for a little less than three hundred dollars.

How did I get such a good deal? *I went shopping!*

But isn't this just dumb luck when you happen across one of these deals that don't come around too often? Well, sometimes it is.

Other times though, I will call the shop and see what kind of deals are coming down the pike. Also, if the regular retail outlets are advertising their big blowout sales, I will usually plan on stopping over at the outlet mall about two to three weeks after the sale because that's usually when the stuff that doesn't sell in the blowout sale ends up at the outlets.

It's as simple as this. If you do not get another set of eyes on the market, you will never truly know what kind of deals are out there. I call it the "Harlem Globetrotters effect." They play exhibitions and know they're supposed to win every night, so do you think they try as hard?

The competition encourages the availability of better deals, but you have to be shopping around to find yourself one.

How to Market Your Insurance Program

So you decide to market your insurance program to see what the market will bear, but how, exactly, does one go about this?

First, you want to be prepared so that when your company is presented to the insurance market, the presentation will put you in the most favorable light. Wait, isn't that the broker's job? Yes, it is, but it's also vital that you sell your company to the broker first, so he is excited about marketing your program to insurance companies.

Begin by gathering up the information. This is easy, since you get a request from the current broker each year for the information they need to roll over your account. The key to the marketing plan, as you well know, is all in the presentation. Let's say you go out to a fancy restaurant and order the best steak on the menu. The waiter brings the meal and serves it to you on a used trash can top. It doesn't matter how hungry you are or how good that steak may be, you will never eat it because of the way it was presented.

To present a professional look, the cover can be set up using desktop publishing software. It should be titled "Risk Management Package" with the year upon which the insurance program is to be quoted. It should include the company name, logo, and a design, which will indicate what type of industry your company is in.

The presentation should be professional in its look, but not too slick as to create the impression that the organization might have extra cash available to buy stuff, like say, extra insurance.

The following information is essential to this presentation:

1. **Overview of the Company**—Start with an overall historical perspective on the company, giving a brief synopsis of the growth of the company along with some useless information, such as the total number of years

of management experience for executives. Business folks seem to like that. You should include the most basic of information such as how long the company has been in business, how it came to be formed, and how it has evolved into the company it is today.

2. **Brief Biographies of Key Executives**—This should be brief and explain the skills and experience each individual brings to the organization. Two paragraphs for owners and a single paragraph for key executives. A word to the wise: Let the executives know that their bio will be no longer than a paragraph. Some will still give you four or five pages, and they will be crushed when it's edited down to a paragraph. Oh, well. Those executives will still be crushed, but at least they were forewarned.

3. **The Risk-Management Function**—Give a brief one-or two-page generic explanation of risk management. It helps to create the impression that you know what this insurance stuff is all about: "At Vinnie's, we strive each and every day to control the risk in all aspects of the organization. The implementation of safety standards complemented by aggressive mitigation of claims allows Vinnie's to achieve the highest degree of risk control." You see what I mean. It really doesn't say much, but it looks like you might know something about this subject, even if you don't.

4. **The Risk-Management Department**—Give an overview of the department. At one company, I was the only one in the risk-management department, so I would proffer this as "The risk management department is headed up by…" If you tell them that your department has a staff of one, the insurers might suspect that your organization is not as serious as you say you are. If you don't have a dedicated risk manager, use the same verbiage for whoever is handling the insurance. If it is the owner or a key executive, make this a part of their biography and follow it up in this section the same way.

5. **Safety Department**—If you don't have a safety department, you should probably get one. A safety department shows a commitment to the safety of your employees, customers, and the general public. Attention to safety goes a long way toward convincing a highly rated insurance carrier that you're a good risk. If you cannot dedicate resources to a safety department, you can make this a function of the security department or the risk management department to emphasize your commitment to safety. A reality-based safety program (as opposed to handling safety

concerns with a fingers-crossed wink-and-a-nod attitude) will improve your loss history, which affects the premiums you pay.

6. **Overview of Your Product or Services**—Let the prospective carriers know what kind of work you do (e.g., the product you produce or the service you provide).

7. **Revenue Reports**—This will show the level of growth the company has seen. The reports should be simple enough to be understood but sophisticated enough to show that your company has a depth of understanding when it comes to business. Do not include a payroll summary or a breakdown of per unit costs. This report is intended to convey the most basic of information and can be supplemented if and when a broker is selected to market the account. These blanks can be filled in later, if necessary.

8. **Insurance Policy History**—Here you provide a list of the insurance policies in force for the past five years. Each policy year should be listed, along with the insurer and policy number, and should be listed in categories by type of insurance. This is helpful in the marketing of your account, so brokers can look up your loss history. It's also pretty important to have this information should a claim arise from a previous year, so you know who to report it to.

9. **Loss History**—This should include the loss information on all policies based on the most current loss runs before the printing of this presentation. This will give those brokers who are interested the opportunity to see the loss history, and if they decide to market the account, they can request current loss runs.

10. **Loss Runs**—Loss runs should be provided to those who are invited to shop the account. If these loss runs are too many pages to include in the body of the presentation, send them along with the risk-management package. It is important that the loss history provided in the report complements the numbers on the loss runs.

Send the presentation out with a cover letter that gives the prospective broker the opportunity to market the account. You should never allow anyone to shop you around if they don't have permission to do so.

An invitation to bid is just that—an invitation. It is not an intent to contract, nor does it create an agency relationship. It simply allows the broker to go to the market on your behalf.

The decision on who can bid the account is up to you. You can send the packages out to anyone who solicits your company for the business; however, this may serve to saturate the market and may not be the best plan, although this strategy generally will cause brokers to narrow their focus to insurers that actually might match your needs.

The best strategy is to research each broker and allow two or three additional brokers to market the account, in addition to the current broker of record. You should let the bidding brokers know that the organization will not be moving the account for pennies, and that only a significant premium reduction would cause a move.

If you have done your homework, service should be a given and should be weighed equally among each participant, although you really don't know what kind of service you are going to get until you move the account over.

Finally, give each prospective bidder a drop-dead date of fifteen days prior to renewal. Request that the final numbers be prepared thirty days out, but absolutely do not accept any numbers after the drop-dead date. If you give the broker three to four months to prepare, and they can't hit a drop-dead date, this is probably indicative of the kind of service they would provide if selected.

Pricing

Be careful when you market the account out for the first time. Some brokers will provide you with quotes without giving information about the carrier. This is not acceptable.

You need to know who the carrier is to determine if that carrier is acceptable to all parties to which your organization is contractually obligated. If the quote does not name the company, you should not consider it. The quote should also include the insurer's A.M. Best rating. This can be found on the A.M. Best Web site. All carriers should be A+ rated or better, although some industries can usually make due with an A-carrier. Anything below A-and you could be asking for trouble.

Each broker will submit quotes that are based on different base units. For example, a general liability quote may be based on direct payroll or perhaps gross revenues. It is important to have at least two weeks so you can quantify these quotes to determine which would be more advantageous to the organization. It's a matter of trying to compare "apples to apples."

If, after you analyze the quotes and determine that the broker of record's quotes are significantly higher, you need to get assurances from the broker with the best numbers that they can handle your needs concerning the distribution of certificates, billing, and financing.

I always make a habit of sharing the quotes verbally with each broker once the numbers have been presented. The reason for this is simple: the brokers will start to pick apart the others' proposals, asking questions like—"Is that an A+ rated carrier?" or "Does the umbrella drop down if the primary insurer goes belly-up?"

If the incumbent broker believes he is about to lose his prime rollover account, he will ask questions to attempt to validate his numbers and disparage the competition. The broker of record will also ask questions that you might not think of, and this will actually help you make the case against him. He will also ask the questions that are essential but you had forgotten to ask.

In the end, if the premium reduction is significant and the issues are answered to your satisfaction, the incumbent broker will generally come down to numbers that are equal or at least competitive with the competition. This proves one thing and one thing only: *your broker has been overcharging you for years!*

It makes the decision to leave your buddy that much easier. Some will even say something like, "You'll be back," which is almost as feeble as the broker who says, "You're due."

More like, "You're done."

A Proactive Approach

Now, you may read this and think it sounds like a lot of work. And the first year it may be. In the following years, however, you are only updating the information for the expiring year and dropping off the history from the fifth year. The administrative portion of this will need a commitment on your part, but it isn't a full-time commitment. Most carriers will e-mail your loss runs to you if you request them.

The financial information can be estimated if this is proprietary information, and you probably need to edit out executives who have left and add their replacements. If something innovative has occurred in the past year—adding a territory, commitment of resources to safety or security, or a new computer system—this should be included and highlighted. The insurance industry likes to see positive growth, and they like to see that their customers are expanding and a good risk to boot.

5

What's the Deal with Lawyers?

Why Lawsuits Can Get Out of Hand

A woman buys a cup a coffee at a drive-through of a popular, national fast-food restaurant. The coffee spills on her lap and burns her thighs, requiring medical attention.

Now what happens next is what makes this case so unbelievable. This older woman seeks medical attention, and the doctors determine that she has third-degree burns on her thighs. She incurs medical bills of approximately $20,000 and asks the fast-food chain to reimburse her for these expenses.

Now, you would think, as a risk manager, I would begin to rage at this woman and at the civil legal system that could allow this case to even come to trial. It is an issue of assumption of risk, isn't it? I mean, a prudent person knows that putting a cup of coffee between their legs in the front seat of a car may lead to an injury of this type, even though the coffee has a lid.

Nope.

According to published reports, the lady's daughter found out about it, and made a claim against the fast-food chain just to get her mom's medical bills paid. At first she was ignored, and then, after a period of time the claim was denied. The daughter eventually secured legal counsel, the case went all the way to trial, and the lady was awarded millions of dollars.

Why, that's outrageous, you say. How could you defend this kind of settlement?

Whoa! I'm certainly not defending the settlement. I *am* saying that the approach that the company took to handle this case caused this result.

They got what they deserved. In my opinion, the company broke the one cardinal rule of risk management. They listened to the one group of people who have the most to gain and the least to lose on the outcome of a trial—*the lawyers!*

"We Can Win This Thing"

Now, I know there is a place for lawyers in the insurance business. Lawyers help to write the insurance policies, defend the policy language, and defend the insurer and insured from any claims made against the policy. And they're pretty good at it; very good, in fact. I use them all the time.

Problems arise, however, when the insurer and insured cede complete authority for the direction of any given claim to the legal team.

Here's a hint: If a lawyer shuffles over and whispers in my ear, "We can win this thing," I immediately start thinking about settling the case. If you are aware of the circumstances of the case and are up to date on the facts, but an attorney tries to convince you to litigate the thing, and you listen to them, then shame on you. This is not about the competence of attorneys—it's all about retaining control over the direction of the case.

The fact that "we can win this case" should have little bearing on the determination to go to trial or not. And if the case reaches the point at which you need legal representation, it has also reached the point at which you don't need convincing as to the need to go to trial or not. It should all be there for you to decide.

Let's look at this fast-food case. For only $20,000, this case could have been settled without impacting the legal system. Or let's just say it was negotiated up to $60,000, which is probably what the case was worth. The fast-food folks offered her eight hundred dollars.

Controlling the Direction of the Case

As an innocent bystander, the injured party, by formula, would be afforded three times her medical bills for pain and suffering. An additional amount could be paid in consideration that the company would not admit fault and the case would remain confidential. If this scenario had occurred, it would have been settled in house by the company or the insurer with a general release and no need for legal representation on either side.

But, this didn't occur, probably due to the arrogance of the company and/or the insurer. Once the case escalated to the point at which litigation could occur, the case had been made public, and the company tried to influence public opinion by publicizing the case as an example of the "sue happy" mentality of the American public. The poor woman who only wanted her medical bills paid was being made out to be the poster child for all that is wrong with the tort liability system in the United States.

Even at this point, the company still had the opportunity to settle this case. Whether the attorneys got greedy, or the company began to believe its own story, no one really knows. The fast-food folks held themselves up as the gatekeepers of the system and justified their actions by stating that if they did not take a stand here, they would be sued for all manner of frivolous claims—as if they really care about that. Their ultimate goal is simply to sell more fast food! In the meantime, the lawyers rack up the billable hours.

So it goes to trial, and the lady gets over $2 million. The company appeals the decision, and she gets a little less, but still probably not enough less to cover the bills of the lawyers hired by the company for the appeal. The case was finally settled and the terms were not disclosed. The company has to issue warnings on the cups and lids. And because of all this, they now have better-made cups and lids and have lowered the temperature of their coffee.

They could have achieved this after settling with the gal for $20,000 and quietly have made the improvements to the product. Instead, they paid out about $2 million with at least that much in legal fees, and still had to make the improvements *and* settle all the cases that came forth from the publicity from the case—same results, for an extra four million dollars.

The Lesson

Don't let lawyers control the direction of the case! Outside counsel is much more competent and experienced with these cases than any in-house counsel would be. These folks have the experience to mitigate, and if necessary, to litigate. Their ultimate goal is to allow the organization to be in the best position to make its best decision. This includes looking at the bigger picture, not just the facts of this one case. The downside of this equation is that outside counsel make more money if the case goes to trial, win or lose. Their bottom line increases only as long as the case continues.

On the other hand, in-house counsel likes to fight cases so they can win "the big one" and use that to get a job with a real law firm. The driving motivation of your counsel may be diametrically opposed to your goal in this case. If it goes away quickly, they make no money. If it goes to trial and they lose, they make more cash on the appeal. That might not be the objective of the organization.

The role of a risk manager in a high-dollar or high-profile case is to make those at the executive level aware of the alternatives in the case. The best and worst case scenarios, as well as the cost of ongoing legal involvement, should be the primary considerations, along with how each action will affect the company's reputation in the marketplace and with the public. Upper management can then make an informed decision based on the "big picture," which takes into account the goodwill and public relations ramifications of their decision.

At this point, before trial is set, every effort should be made to settle the case.

If negative publicity is an issue, the case can be resolved with a confidentiality agreement, which may cost more, but will give the organization a better opportunity to mitigate the loss than would a three-week trial that is one of the top stories on the major broadcast networks as well as every cable news outlet for a month straight.

Well, you say, what if they are making an outrageous demand? Well, you should still make every attempt to settle. This is not like some one-hour TV drama in which the parties show up on Wednesday to sue, and the case goes to trial the following Monday.

The high-dollar cases generally take from two to four years to get to the trial stage. This gives all involved an opportunity to assess the relative value of the case, the amount being offered for settlement, and if the disparity is too big, the relative value of going before a jury.

One thing most companies fail to realize through all this is that the plaintiff is risking it all by going to court too! Most plaintiff attorneys work these cases on a contingency basis, meaning that they pay for the investigation, motions, depositions, and interrogatories, and they get paid only if they win. Their payment is based on a percentage of the settlement or award. If they lose, they get nothing.

Most lawyers I know are pretty intelligent and would not risk going unpaid for their work. The longer the legal process drags on, the more money the plaintiff lawyer invests, and the lower end of his or her settlement threshold begins to fall.

An organization should always be prepared to litigate, but only as a last resort. Conversely, a plaintiff should attempt to get the best deal without going to trial as well. Losing the case outright is not in the client's or attorney's best interest.

If the case nears trial and there is a significant difference between the offer your side makes and what the other party wants, you should factor in the price of a trial and put that cash on the table to attempt to close the gap.

You should be able to settle the case for less than the amount you would have to pay the lawyers, whom *you* pay whether you win or not.

Now, once you absorb the information to this point, you must understand the one basic premise of your attorney/client relationship: your attorneys are on your side. They work for you!

The Lessons Learned

Let's now take a look at the attorneys on the other side. These are the guys and gals who claim injury, illness, or insult to their client whose direct or proximate cause was the negligence of you or your employee.

There are two basic reasons why someone would bring a lawsuit against your organization:

1. Breach of contract

2. Any other civil wrong that is not a breach of contract (tort)

Most risk managers/insurance professionals deal primarily with tort liability, which is injury caused by your intent, recklessness, negligence, or liability without fault (strict liability).

Tort liability provides for compensation for a wrong, which may include physical or emotional injury, loss of reputation, libel, slander, and so forth.

Although people commit wrongs for which there is no practical remedy (a wrongful death suit cannot bring back the dead), the law provides for a specific remedy for all wrongs—money.

The law places a dollar value on all kinds of losses, and the legal system awards or allows for negotiation of compensation in the form of damages.

These damages compensate the injured party for loss due to the other party's negligence (compensatory damages).

If the negligent party (defendant) acts in a particularly bad manner, the injured party (plaintiff) can be awarded additional cash to punish the defendant for this egregious behavior (punitive damages).

There is an industry of lawyers out there who cater to tort liability clientele. You've seen them on the late night TV commercials: "Do you have a phone? Then I'll be your lawyer."

These are the folks who would drive me nuts when I was handling auto liability claims. I actually had a guy who was rear-ended by one of our renters. He got out of the car and said everything was fine—not a scratch on either vehicle. As soon as he found out it was a rental car, he started to complain that his back hurt and called the police. It was as though our cars had big dollar signs on them.

It is commonly understood that you never know the extent of your injuries until you speak with your lawyer.

What is not so commonly known is that there is an ancillary industry of doctors and health-care providers who will treat these so-called injured parties whether they are injured or not.

Why would they do such a thing? The lawyer doesn't profit from additional medical treatment. Wouldn't medical fees take away from the attorney's cut of the settlement? Well, yes and no. The accepted formula for insurance companies is that the settlement for the emotional toll and nontangible losses from an injury (pain and suffering) is three times the medical bills (medicals).

For example, if a plaintiff has $10,000 in medical bills (special damages), he or she can reasonably expect to receive $20,000 in a settlement just for pain and suffering (specials × 3, for a total claim value of $30,000).

Insurance companies usually put the ultimate value of this particular case at $30,000 using this formula while the plaintiff attorney will argue that the three-times-the-medicals rule is pain and suffering only and that the medical bills should be paid in addition. Thus, their interpretation puts the value at $40,000: $10,000 for the bills and $30,000 for pain and suffering.

Most plaintiff attorneys will eventually settle somewhere in the middle, absent of any extenuating circumstances such as punitive damages or the value added by making the settlement confidential. The bottom line: the higher the medical bills, the higher the anticipated settlement.

This is only a standard guideline. Mitigating factors and negotiations will pull that number up or bring it down, based on whether the plaintiff contributed to the circumstances that caused the injury or whether they put themselves in a situation in which they knew the risk of injury was great (assumption of risk).

An example of this is when someone gets into a vehicle with an obviously inebriated driver and then sues for injury when the driver crashes. A reasonable person knows that the chances of crashing are pretty good when getting into a vehicle driven by a seriously drunk driver, and that passenger has the choice of getting in the car or not. Assumption of risk generally tends to lower the value of the claim.

I had one case that exemplified the egregious nature of this tort liability cottage industry. One of the rental vehicles backed into a cab attempting to exit the terminal at the local airport, injuring the wife of the cabbie, who was sitting in the front seat of the taxi at the time of the impact.

The case went to trial (I actually was asked to appear as the representative of the leasing company; our company had no exposure in the case), and our attorney tore into the plaintiff's specialist, getting him to admit that he really couldn't find anything wrong with the cabbie's wife. He then tried to explain why he had scheduled five MRIs over a two-week period and repeated the testing with three more MRIs two months later. The jury got the case late in the day, so I left and asked the attorney to call me when the jury came back.

"What's your prediction? I think we'll win it outright," my attorney said.

"$20 to $25K," I replied.

The jury came back with an award of $22,000.

How did I know? Am I a great psychic or an incredibly intelligent human being? Not really. The answer, though, shows what's wrong with this system today in the United States.

The jury did not believe that the extent of the injury was more than a bump on the head. Our questioning had proven to them that the treating physician was a quack.

But the lady had over $15,000 in specials (medical bills, rental car, lost income), and the jury looked at her as the victim of an overzealous attorney who had run up the bills to pad the case.

In their minds, she would have been stuck with all those medical bills if they hadn't awarded her the damages. So they gave her enough to cover her medical bills and enough to make it worth her while without giving too much to the lawyer.

Thus the $22K. The plaintiff walked away with about $3,000 after the attorney took his piece and added any out-of-pocket expenses he incurred. The attorney paid the medical bills with the rest of the settlement (which is usually charged at a discounted rate, by the way).

It certainly wasn't worth the time she had invested getting all those needless medical tests done, but pretty good for an injury that probably required an ice-pack, two ibuprofen, and a bandage.

On another occasion I received a letter of representation from a lawyer representing a gal who had rented a car from us and was hit by another vehicle. The other party was at fault.

I was trying to get a copy of the police report so I could collect for the damage to the rental vehicle. I dialed his number and heard his greeting: "This is Attorney Joe Jones. I am not available to take your call right now. If you are calling in regards to a settlement, press one. For all other matters, press two."

I hit two and left a message. No response.

I called again, hit two, and left a message. Again, no response.

This went on for about three weeks. I shared this dilemma with an attorney friend of mine, and he told me to just hit one and see what happened.

Genius.

I got back to the office, called the number, and pressed one. I left my name, the case I was calling about, and my number. The attorney called me back about ten minutes later.

"Hello, you're calling in regards to a settlement?"

"Hey, Mr. Jones, thanks for calling me back. I was wondering if you could fax me a copy of the police report...."

"So...you're not calling in regards to a settlement...." He proceeded to go off on me, saying he was going to sue both me and my company. He was really mad.

I never got that police report from him, but I did have the opportunity to release some pent-up anxiety on him, and I got a good lawyer story to boot.

Another thing I like to do concerns depositions. Now, there is really no reason to bring in the owner's representative in a third party negligence case, but if an attorney is willing to waste his time (and money), I am going to give him his money's worth.

During one of the first depositions I did, I was asked by an attorney to shorten my answers. There were eight attorneys representing seven different interests, and they were all hunting for a way into my company's pocket.

I asked him that if he knew the length of my answers beforehand, then why did he need me to testify? I was out of there about ten minutes later. I think they said something about a tee time.

In another case, an attorney was grilling me pretty good, to the point of getting nasty. So I went into my "I have no personal recollection of that instance" routine (because I rarely see any of the accidents that bring about these cases). The attorney asked the court stenographer to go off the record and then floored me when he looked over to the stenographer and said, "What a scumbag!"

He then went right back on the record and asked me to answer another question. I told him that I would but that, before I did, I wanted to say on the record that while we were off the record, Mr. Smith had referred to me as a scumbag.

The stenographer started coughing in a feeble attempt to muffle her laughter. I hope she got paid for that day.

As I was leaving, I told my attorney that he did not have the authority to settle this case without my approval. We dragged the case out until the opposing attorney withdrew. We settled directly with the other party.

Come to think of it, maybe I am a scumbag.

This is exactly why tort reform is such a big issue today. It is also why tort reform will never occur. Because on both sides of the equation are lawyers, attorneys, barristers,...whatever you want to call them.

A lawsuit is a game of cat and mouse, and every move is intended to increase or decrease the value of the case. It's not for the faint of heart.

One more thing about those guys who advertise on TV: I actually like dealing with them. Why? Well, these firms tend to be claims mills in which paralegals are hired to settle cases. These firms profit off of the volume. Quantity instead of quality.

I have generally been able to settle these cases for lower than the actual value because these firms are eager to settle, get their commission, and move on to the next case.

The Skinny on Attorneys

Lawyers are a necessary part of business. The degree of control you have in a liability claim depends entirely on who is paying the attorney (go figure). If you are self-insured and hired the law firm directly, you have absolute authority over the actions they take on your behalf. If it's the insurance company's dime, you will have some influence on the direction of the case, but the ultimate decision is up to the insurer, unless you're willing to kick in some cash above and beyond your insurance premium, which I have never done and do not advocate.

Remember, just as the plaintiff's attorney worries about losing the case at trial, insurance companies know they must pay for the consequences of any action they pursue, and they are pretty good about minimizing their costs. And...

That's Why Most Cases Settle

6
Do You Hate Claims As Much As I Do?

A Sobering Reality

I had a claim once. In fact, I've had a lot of claims.

One time, when I was in my early twenties, I was looking at the traffic light as it turned green. Unfortunately, it was the light at the next intersection. I proceeded into the intersection, and just as I saw the car cross in front of me, I realized I had made a terrible error in judgment. I can still see the look on that little old lady's face just before impact. I wasn't going that fast, but it was enough to jostle her, and her vehicle, an older model Buick, just kind of rolled aimlessly through the intersection, across the sidewalk, and came to a stop after grazing the side of a schoolhouse. The cops came; the ambulance came; and I was given a ticket for something or another (although I did get out and say something profound like, "The light was green, wasn't it?"). I was able to drive my vehicle home—well, almost home. The engine actually fell down below the wheel area (motor mounts, they said), which seriously impeded the progress to my destination.

The best part of the story: I was taking a shortcut through town.

I gave the police my insurance information. I had just received the card from my new agent, who had written the new policy about three weeks earlier. I hope he got his commission.

Three days later, I got a call from the insurance adjuster who was assigned to my claim. Now, this guy was a piece of work. He seemed really mad that he had to handle this case for someone who was insured with his company and had the audacity to be at fault in an accident. I was sure it was because the policy was new and his company lost a lot of cash insuring me. Turns out he just had a bad attitude.

He couldn't have cared less that I had totaled both my car and the little old lady's car and that she had been hauled away in an ambulance. And he wasn't upset because he had to talk to some irresponsible young kid with a high-pitched voice.

No, he was ticked off because he was a claims adjuster.

Claims folk are a rare breed. They all seem to start their careers ready to take on the world, looking into every crevice to discover a wisp of fraud, dedicating their lives to the eradication of false claim activities. Then, once they're in the business for a while, they move up to management, where they still have to deal with claims, but for the most part they don't have to deal directly with the public.

Hey, who can blame them for wanting to move? People are generally at their best and most courteous when they have a claim.

Sure.

Then, if they're smart, they transfer to another department. If they're lucky, they can move into underwriting, where there is absolutely no human interaction whatsoever.

Most claims folks don't do well moving into underwriting due to their deep-rooted anger toward all the insured humans who did them wrong while they were in claims.

This tends to reflect in their pricing of the insurance product, which tends to lead to a loss in business, which in turn lands the former adjuster back into claims, where he or she turns over files and deals with little snot-nosed kids with high-pitched voices who try to kill little old ladies after only being insured for less than a month.

Bitter? I'd guess yes. Anyway, I digress. There are two types of insurance claims:

1. The first is the type where the insurance company protects your interest because of a claim arising from your negligence (liability or third party claim).

A good example is when you run a red light you think is green and you come to hit some little old lady who sues you because she is really, really sore.

2. The second comes when you make a claim because something you insure becomes damaged (first party claim). A good example of this is the amount your insurance company pays you for the damage done to your car. You might also file a first party claim for repairing or replacing parts of your house that are damaged due to wind, hail, or some other peril covered on your policy.

There are first party claims and third party claims: where the heck did the second party go? If you have wondered about this but have been afraid to ask because you thought you were supposed to know, here's how it goes:

- ***The first party in a claim is you.*** The other party is the first party for their own claim (if this confuses, forget the second part). From your standpoint, there is only one first party.

- ***The third party is the other party who is making a claim against you as the first party.*** There can be more than one third party although each third party is referred to as a third party, and not the fourth party, fifth party, and so forth. I think the reason for this is ego, or that the third party may be understood to have a higher priority than the fourth or fifth party. Or it may be for some totally different reason. Regardless, I have had to change and reprint accident reports because the person filling out the report has put "N/A" or "None" in the box that read "Third Party," stating that there were only two parties involved.

- ***The ever-elusive second party***, which is never referred to, is generally understood to be the insurance company that is representing the interests of the first party.

This being said, claims are a fact of life, whether or not you are in business. In business, there will be losses, and there will be occasions when someone will claim that their loss is your fault. The thing about claims is that you never know when one is going to occur, so you really can't plan for them, right?

Wrong.

Claims administration is the aspect of insurance that needs the most planning and management to maximize the collection potential and minimize the loss potential.

I once heard of a homeowners association near me that actually tried to restrict the public from access to sidewalks and pathways within the homeowners association after it became a party to a small liability lawsuit. This backfired. Because there is nothing that precludes a homeowner claiming negligence from initiating an action against the association through the board, the restriction only invited more lawsuits. They actually started carding people walking down the street.

"Hey, do you live here? OK, then, I'll need some identification."

Why were they doing this? Because they didn't have a clue, that's why. If they wanted to spend money on security, why not buy some better advice, for goodness' sake. In effect, the association walked into a building, and when a lightbulb blew out, they tore down the building.

Claims happen. That's the beauty of living in the United States: anyone is free to sue anyone for anything. It is up to the parties involved to settle the matter, and if they are unable to do so, the court will decide based on the merits of the case.

So instead of reacting with shock and surprise, you need to have a plan of action that maximizes the potential for collecting losses against your property caused by other parties and defending liability claims made against you, which will help to mitigate (lessen) the losses you may incur. If you don't have a plan for claims administration and direction, you'll lose a lot of money.

Strategies to Help You Along

I have found that the key to handling claims and claims personnel is having an appreciation for the claims adjuster's job and an understanding of what he or she goes through each and every day.

I think that most adjusters will agree that people are kind, fair, and courteous when interacting with an insurance company due to a claim—that is, until the insurance company says no. That's generally when things get ugly.

Claimants are like your kids. If they ask for something and you say yes really quickly, they see an opportunity to ask for something else. If you say yes to that, they will go for the hat trick and continue to go down the list of desires until you say no. It doesn't matter how many times you say yes, as soon as you say no, you hear, "But why not?"

This same happens with insurance claims departments:

"Here's the estimate. Are you going to send me a check?"

"Sure. It will be in the mail today."

"OK, are you going to pay the rental car bill?"

"Sure, pay for it and send me the bill."

"They only had an Escalade left. Is that OK? It's only $99.95 per day."

"Yeah, don't worry about it."

"Will you pay for my mother-in-law's bunion surgery, which the health insurer won't pay because it's elective, and, by the way, what's up with that?"

"Uh, no."

"Well, you'll hear from my lawyer in the morning. You insurance companies are all alike…you #@!*"

As an aside, I do need to ask two questions: how is it that so many people have their own lawyers, and where can I sign up for one of those? They always refer to their lawyer as "my lawyer," just like on all those legal eagle shows.

Well, they really don't.

In all my years handling claims, whenever someone said they were going to get their lawyer on the case, I would end the conversation by saying I wasn't allowed to speak to them further except in the presence of their lawyer. Most would call back in an hour or two and confess that they really didn't have an attorney and that their sister-in-law had told them to say that. They're generally a little more reasonable once they realize that you saw that episode too.

When dealing with liability claims, most companies are inclined to report the claim to the insurer and let them handle it from there. In truth, I really couldn't be bothered with liability claims follow-up until I began to administer a self-insured program and my organization paid every dime.

Only once you get charged by your third party administrator to send someone down to get a police report (at $40 per hour) or you pay an attorney and three associates for a day of depositions do you truly begin to realize the value of assisting the insurer in any way possible to lessen the financial blow of that loss.

There is a "best way" to work liability claims:

- Use the resources within your organization to collect as much information as possible for the insurer to sufficiently protect your interests. Insurers love it when you get involved in this way and will actually begin to encourage input from you when you have other claims that come against you. If you are in an organization that has a fair amount of claims activity, and you stay for a few years with the same insurer, you are generally going to interact with the same adjusters. If you help them do their job more efficiently, they will be more inclined to fight a little harder on your behalf because of the effort you put in—especially if your information helps them.

- Make sure that you communicate any information as soon as you receive it. The longer a claim lingers, the greater the expectations from the other side. If you uncover information that would serve to mitigate your loss, give it up to your adjuster as soon as you know about it and make sure you explain the value of the information if it is not immediately apparent.

- Do not withhold any information from the insurance adjuster that you feel may be potentially damaging to you, especially if you know this information is going to come out any way. It's best that they hear it from you first. For example, whenever I make a major error at work (obviously, I have and I do), I will tell my bosses about it immediately and I don't try to bury it. First of all, they are entitled to that information, and if it's going to come out, I have the opportunity to give them my explanation first. In fact, my story becomes the story, and I don't have to defend myself from someone else's take on the situation. It also prevents my bosses from getting blindsided. Oh yeah, it's also the right thing to do.

- Maintain your credibility with the insurer by providing all the information you have that can assist them in protecting your interests. Communicate with the adjuster for updates but don't waste the adjuster's time calling every day when there has been no change in the case. There is a thin line between communicating and being a pain in the butt, and, if you think you are close to that line, don't make the call.

Now, when you are working third party claims, this is called subrogation. My wife once asked me a long time ago whether *subrogation* was really a word or just something the insurance companies made up. I told her it really was a word but I wasn't sure what it meant.

Well, this is what it means: subrogation is an equitable doctrine holding that when a third party pays a creditor or obligee, the third party succeeds to the creditor's rights against the debtor or obligor.

Ha-ha-ha! Gotcha! You never know when that old insurance language is going to creep up on you.

In plain English, it means that if I pay you back for something someone else owes you, I have the right to go after that other party for the loss I paid you. So, if the insurance company pays you for a loss that is someone else's fault, they can then collect that debt back from the at-fault (negligent) party. You can't collect from the insurer and then try to collect from the other party as well.

The insurance company, when called upon, takes your place and defends you. That's why the insurer is the great unknown "second party."

Subrogation in insurance is also, rightly or wrongly, the term used by the business community when the organization pursues a third party that it perceives to have been negligent. They do this because it sounds cool and because no one generally wants to do collections (which is really what this is). But they are willing to subrogate. That's how I ended up in the insurance business.

Anatomy of an Insurance Adjuster

Although there are no real rules to claiming a loss against a third party or the third party's insurer, there are some valuable tools to help you get what you are asking for in a timely manner.

First, you need to understand that being an adjuster is not the best job in the world. People yell and scream and ask for more than they are actually entitled to—and that's just the adjuster's family. Seriously, though, if you understand what the adjuster has to deal with each day, it will help you better formulate a strategy for getting your claims paid.

First, you have to get this notion out of your head that your adjuster is just waiting for you to call and that your claim is the only one he has, so he should sit there and listen to you dump on him because his insured screwed up.

The good adjusters, however, *will* create the impression that yours is their only claim and that even if he or she had another claim, yours would be the most important. But this is definitely not the case.

So, what is the best way to deal with adjusters? Help them out. Don't get upset or huffy, but stand firm with your claim. These folks are only doing their job, and they tend to get yelled at by the insured…

"What do you mean I have a $1,000 deductible? Nobody told me that."

And third parties…

"Rot in hell, Satan. I'll see you in court."

And third party attorneys…

"Pay this amount and then rot in hell, Satan!"

And even their wives…

"If you work late again tonight, you might as well rot in hell, Shelton!"

In the course of a twenty-year career, adjusters tune this anger out about… oh, one week after becoming a claims adjuster. So if you call up an adjuster and raise hell with him, it's bound to get you absolutely nowhere. On the other hand, if you show even the least amount of empathy and understanding for the job they have to do, you are more apt to get your claim resolved quickly and to your satisfaction.

In the following section, I have tried to paint a picture of what adjusters go through daily. If you know what they are up against, you are more than likely to have the foundation necessary to get the adjuster to pay your claim in a timely manner. Here goes.

A Day in the Life

First and foremost, claims departments are on the lower end of the food chain in the hierarchy of an insurance company. Like risk management in the business community, claims is not the glamorous end of the business

Generally, the claims department will be separated out from the other company departments because no one wants to see the carnage that their internal policies and procedures have brought upon the organization.

Have you ever noticed this? Even if the rest of the departments are in the same building, they cannot access claims whatsoever. More often than not, though, they put the claims department in a separate building to limit the other departments' interaction with the public.

Second, and most important, when an insurance company is looking to downsize and reduce payroll, it tends to look at the claims department first and make its cuts there. This is generally done so that management does not have to see the results of its downsizing.

Downsizing is generally not done because the work has tailed off. In fact, insurance companies often experience cash shortfalls due to the increased claim activity brought on by natural events or the inadequate standards set by underwriting that causes the increased claims activity. So, when claims positions are cut, the workload has generally increased and the increased workload has to be spread across fewer claims staff members.

The adjusters who are not sent packing are relieved for about an hour until the inevitable meeting is held to divide up the work of the released adjusters to those who are left behind. Each adjuster must not only assume the new cases that should have been assigned to adjusters who are no longer there, they have to take over all the old claims that have recently been opened, those that are in the middle of negotiations, and, of course, those that are getting close to settling or going to court. This in turn hinders their ability to settle not only the new cases but also the cases they had previously been assigned and were working prior to the downsizing.

After downsizing, insurance adjusters have to deal with even more people who have become frustrated with the process, because the person they were dealing with before is gone and the new person doesn't have a clue about the facts of their case and doesn't seem to care.

And it's not that they don't care. Well, actually, they usually don't, but they also do not have the time to handle their caseload *and* the additional assigned open cases *and* the increased workload from the allocation of the new claims.

And then you call!

Fred

Let's call our imaginary adjuster Fred. He answers the phone to find that you are attempting to subrogate a property damage claim for a loss due to the negligence of Fred's insured.

It really doesn't matter that you believe that your claim is the most important thing going in your life, and he certainly doesn't want to hear your life story. Fred couldn't care less.

All Fred really wants is to stop that ringing in his ears, which is directly caused by the telephones ringing at his desk and the other adjusters' desks, as well as the constant noise coming from the desks of those who were in the office yesterday but are now just a memory. He once shared lunch with these folks and talked with them about his kids and their grandkids, and now that they are gone forever, leaving only the constant ringing of their extension behind (which management has on four rings before the message comes on, telling the caller that that adjuster has "left the company" and "if you need to speak to someone, dial this extension and ask for Fred, the new adjuster on your case…"). So Fred can count the seconds that the other extension stops ringing, and his extension begins to ring.

One more thing: just like me, Fred has all his open claims in various piles and no one is privy to his system, which is probably the only reason Fred made the cut. No one wanted to go in and figure out Fred's intricate system of piles and piles of files. This is a technique that I like to call "stack management." None of the piles are labeled, yet Fred seems to be able to go to any of his piles to pick out the file he needs to access.

As a matter of fact, he tests out his system from time to time when he takes a few days off and someone from the office calls looking for one of his files. Despite his description of where the file is located in his office, no one can find it.

When he returns, his coworkers give him grief about his lack of organization, at which time, before he even puts down his bag, he reaches into one of the stacks and pulls out the file they so desperately sought.

It drives people nuts.

The bosses have the following conversation when it comes time to downsize:

"Well, we could probably lose Fred; no one would care if he was gone."

"Oh, no you don't. Have you ever seen his office? He's the only one who knows where anything is."

"OK, we'll keep Fred."

And for one short moment, Fred wins. And then…more piles arrive. Piles and piles of new as well as ongoing claims.

So, when you call, what is your goal? You have to somehow motivate Fred to find your file from the stack in which he has it stashed to the stack on his immediate left on his desk. From there, you need to motivate him to take that file from wherever it is in that stack of working claims and move it to the top of the aforementioned stack so it can be considered, valued, and paid.

Breaking Down the Claim Package

How does one accomplish this? Actually, it's fairly simple, and it's a good strategy for claims, audits, attorneys, or anyone else impeding your path to that short-term goal. Create a claim package that includes the following:

- A **cover letter** explaining the reason for the package in clear and concise language. This letter should explain why you have an interest in the claim (e.g., owner of the vehicle, parent of the injured employee, a company representative); what loss you are claiming (description of property) and why you feel the other party is responsible (e.g., "Our investigation reveals that your insured is at fault"); the address where the payment should be sent; and a telephone number at which you can be reached.

- An **estimate of repair or repair/replacement order**—paperwork substantiating the real (tangible) loss you have incurred

- A backup for any **additional charges** (e.g., rental car, taxis to the doctor, child care for doctor visits).

- A **police report or other substantiation** for the claim based on the negligence of the other party. Other documents can include a statement from the insured or your representative or agent.

- **An itemization summary**—summary of all tangible and intangibles you may have such as property damage, loss of use, or diminished value. Each charge should be itemized, and the total amount on the bottom of the itemization summary should match the amount claimed on the cover letter.

Remember! You must be able to substantiate what you are claiming. If you itemize something, you must be able to justify it. For example, in an auto claim, if you are claiming loss of use, substantiate the loss from the estimate of repairs, especially if you have a lot of automobile property damage claims. The rule of thumb used to be one week of rental for each $1,000 worth of damage. Some insurance adjusters will try to use five, but will generally accept seven. If it takes you two weeks to get the vehicle into the shop, it is not the insurance company's responsibility to pay the difference due to your indifference.

A claim for losses should be a good faith attempt to make you whole from the loss incurred by the negligence of the other party. That said, you should remember that claims are subjective by nature, and, because of this, the insurance company may be inclined to negotiate the settlement of a property loss. In some instances, they may actually pay the loss from the package you send if the claim appears to be fair and equitable. For both of these reasons, your claim needs to be defensible.

Be prepared to have the claim denied, negotiated, or even paid in full. If you are forced to negotiate or litigate the claim, you cannot ask for more than the amount of the initial claim.

Many organizations do not understand that despite the apparent reasonableness as to the negligence and value of a particular claim, the other party or their insurer may claim mitigating circumstances that would cause the other party to reduce the value of the claim or deny it altogether.

This is what I often hear:

"If they're at fault, sue the bastards!"

"There's no way we can take that amount. It was their fault!"

A wise old guy I worked for long ago gave me this bit of advice the first time I had a claim with obvious and complete liability on the part of the other party, and the insurer was offering much less:

"It's better to get 50% of something than 100% of nothing."

The numbers tend to bear this out:

If you have a $5,000 loss in which the insured is willing to pay except for $200 loss of use and will not cut the check unless you sign a release, you may lose that $5,000 offer in the pursuit of the $200 to which you feel your company is entitled. But, if you take the $5,000 and put it in the bank, the interest and use value of the money paid will generally wash with the amount you are giving up.

You may also find that your attempt to collect the entire amount at the expense of a smaller amount of the overall claims will prompt the insurer to take the offer completely off the table. At that point, you would probably need to turn it over to a collection company, who will take anywhere from 30 to 50 percent of the claim on a contingency basis, based on the age of the case (the older the case, the lower the odds of collecting and thus the higher the contingency percentage). In that case, you will really be settling for less than the amount offered in the beginning, and you will have lost the use of that money, because the loss will have been incurred and paid for a year or two.

Third party claim collections are a funny business. No two claims are exactly alike, yet most take on some of the same characteristics. Some claimants will actually lie to cover a negligent action, and then the burden of proving the obvious becomes yours. It's more or less a game of poker. In poker, you may have the best hand, but you may not have the stomach or the financial capacity to play that hand because of the perception of the other party's hand. If that other party is the 800-pound gorilla we call an insurance company, the poker game can get very old very fast.

If you have a large volume of collection claims, it is valuable to aggressively pursue all avenues of collections. It is not in your best interest, however, to collect from your insurance company, even if the loss is covered. This will drive up your insurance premium at renewal.

The best collection strategy is to go after the party at fault, if one exists. Generally, the at-fault party will have insurance or will be willing to settle directly with you so it doesn't go against their insurance policy.

This will occur only when fault is determined beyond dispute by all parties. Sometimes (a lot of times, in fact), you will find that there are differing views of the same reality (the stories differ), which casts the negligence of the other party in doubt. In these instances, the investigation and footwork you do at the beginning of a loss will not only allow the insurance company to defend your side of the case, it will also provide you with documentation should a third party try to lie their way out of fault.

I know. I know...who would lie in such a case? How could anyone do anything but the right thing when a loss occurs? Difficult as it is to believe, there are many people who will say anything to get out of a loss, for a multitude of reasons:

- They weren't supposed to be where they were, and they don't want their parents to find out.

- They were with someone they weren't supposed to be with, and they don't want their spouse to find out.

- They just know that this last accident will cause their insurance company to cancel their coverage.

- They like to lie.

For whatever reason, some people will not tell the entire truth.

Consider this. Let's say you're driving down the street and someone rear-ends your car. You both get out, and although there is damage to the other car, there is no damage to your vehicle except for a minor scuff mark. The other guy says he will take care of his damage, and, because there is no damage to your vehicle, you just continue on your journey.

Later that evening, you get a knock on the door and it's the local police. It turns out that they received a report that you caused a hit-and-run accident. The other guy said your car had backed into his vehicle while the other vehicle was parked and then the report said you took off. Suddenly, you are facing not only the damage to the other vehicle and a possible injury claim—you are also facing criminal charges for leaving the scene of an accident.

You think this is far-fetched. I've actually seen three cases in which this has happened, or at least our driver made the allegation that this has happened.

Three cases!

The moral of the story is this: if a loss occurs, and it is due to the negligence of another party, call the police! Even if the police don't take a report, the call is still logged and can be verified by the police department later as to the location and circumstances of the incident or accident. Most folks aren't bright enough to make up a lie before the police get there, or stupid enough to try and spin the tale while you're still standing there.

Why Everyone Loves Collection Agencies

At some time, you will need to give up on trying to collect a claim, at which time you need to employ someone who will assist you with collection. There are a few ways you can go about this, none of which is financially attractive.

If you have a relatively low volume of uncollectible claims and your business is primarily local, you may want to employ a local attorney to assist you in the collection of these losses.

There is one important thing to remember: collection and subrogation is where most lawyers start their careers to generate income to assist them in getting a better lawyer job. The advantage to this is you generally have a lot of young, aggressive, hungry lawyers who are willing to work these cases to conclusion.

The most glaring disadvantage to this arrangement is that most of these attorneys are not very experienced. Therefore, they have a tendency to litigate rather than negotiate. To them, litigating is much more fun than negotiating.

The other biggest disadvantage to local attorneys is that they do not have the resources to file all their court motions, so they will ask you to fund any expenses they incur before settlement, as well as pay them a percentage of the final amount.

There is one other thing to remember: younger, inexperienced attorneys will ditch their collection business as soon as something better comes along. Just because they get a judgment does not mean they will be able to collect the judgment. I don't think that part is covered on the bar exam. Putting a lien on property is only actionable once the property is sold. By that time, they are on to more exciting things—like anything else but collections—and you are left watching the pot.

This is why there are collection agencies.

Remember, files should be turned over to collection only when there is only a limited chance of collecting the loss yourself. Most collection companies work on the same premise: they work on a contingency basis, which means that they will take between 30 and 50 percent of any amount they are able to collect. This may sound like a rip-off to you, but if you have gotten nowhere with the claim and it appears to have no chance of going anywhere, a small percentage of something is a lot better than a large percentage of nothing.

In the beginning of my career, I let my ego get in the way of my collection efforts. I would hold and work claims sometimes for 12 to 18 months before sending them to collections. The older the claim gets, however, the harder it is to collect. A collection company will also charge a higher contingency rate if the claim is sent to them after a certain amount of time.

Most of the collection companies I worked with would take 33 percent of any claims sent less than a year old and 50 percent for any file sent that was greater than a year old. Although I knew the age of the claim weighed heavily on the chances of anything being collected, I still held them too long.

For the last ten years, I have sent claims off for collections within 60 to 90 days after aggressively working the claims during the initial period. Not only did I get better results from the files I turned over, my overall collection ratio improved dramatically.

So, how does a company go about choosing a collection agency? First, the agency should have a working knowledge of your industry as well as experience in the states in which you do business.

If you are like me, you are constantly bombarded with collection companies soliciting your business. If the company passes the industry knowledge test and I am interested in using them, I will generally give them three types of claims:

1. A small straightforward claim that I could have collected myself. If it's a small case, you will lose much less on a contingency fee than you would if you hired a company that wasn't really any good at collections. If they can't collect on this case, you should end the relationship.

2. A midsized case that can be collected but will involve a degree of negotiation to get it done. This is a file I haven't been able to collect because I haven't been able to get the other party's attention.

3. A big claim with little or no chance of collection. You tell them up front if they pull this one off, they *will* be getting more business.

Now, I know, you have had cases in which you have worked and worked a claim and have hit a brick wall. You finally send it to collections. They send one letter and the file is settled in full. Don't beat yourself up over this. Some parties just won't react until they know its been kicked up a level, and nothing short of turning it over for collection will get them to move.

It's All in How You Relate

Remember—the business of claims and claims collection is all about relationships. If you know who you are dealing with and assist them with their needs as it pertains to your claim, you will find that your files will be more successfully worked than those of other companies, regardless of whether they are first party (yours) or third party (the other side's) claims. Most of the folks you deal with have the authority to give you everything you are asking for. The key is finding out what will prompt them to do so—*and then do it!*

7

Self-Insurance/No Insurance—What's the Difference?

Alternative Risk Financing

At some point as your organization grows, you will begin to feel the pangs of insurance costs gnawing at your gut. The questions begin to grind on you constantly:

What can I do to get these costs down?

Am I being taken to the cleaners?

Boy, that seems high. Does that sound high to you?

So you call up your broker and ask what you can do to get those pesky costs down. Their reply:

"Well, you know, although it's been a soft market for the past ten years, the market is beginning to show trends that it's going to harden, and insurance costs are going to skyrocket."

or

"Why don't we meet for lunch, and we can discuss it."

Whatever they open with, it leads to a lengthy diatribe with loads and loads of insurance-speak, until they lull you into a sense that all this insurance junk is so complicated that it's worth all the money you're paying them for this stuff. Because you were completely lost after the first 30 seconds, you begin to lose all interest in insurance. At that point, you will tell this guy anything just to get him off the phone. After about five minutes, you just want him to go away. The thought of lunch with these people makes you nauseous. I mean, they are personable and all that, but all they talk about is insurance.

Sure, they ask about the wife and kids. Sure, they tell you about their kids, away at college, hiking through Europe, while he spends his weekends at the country club or on his 50-foot boat with his second wife, Trixie. You know this is going to happen, but at some point you bite the bullet, give these broker folks a call, and plead with them:

"Is there any way to bring these costs down?"

"No—my kid's got two more years at Harvard. Ha-ha! (pause) Ha-ha-ha! Well, OK. Are you interested in self-insuring?"

And so it goes.

To Most People, Self-Insurance Is No Insurance

And, in some cases, it is.

There are many financing options you can use that will help to minimize your insurance costs. To do so, you must have a handle on the frequency and severity of your claims, and you must be able to absorb the losses for which you are responsible. Face it; if you agree to pay these losses yourself, you have to pay these losses yourself.

To feel comfortable with the increased risk, you need ask yourself two questions:

- Can I actually predict my future losses with any degree of certainty?

- Does my organization have the discipline to handle the flexibility and inherent lack of predictability that occurs when turning away from the traditional insurance model? (e.g., Can you handle it when the losses are 10 percent of the insurance premium you would be paying one month, yet are 200 percent of that number the next month?)

Instead of turning claims over to the insurance company and letting them handle them, you, the insured, are responsible for paying a portion of these claims yourself. Don't get me wrong, there is significant cost-saving potential, and your eyes will bug out when you see the numbers—initial numbers that tend to cloud your thinking when you are trying to make an informed decision.

The up-front numbers, especially in the first year, are not indicative of the overall savings generated by self-funding. The first-year numbers are actually better, much better. The rest is up to you because you are not funding any losses from previous years that come due in the first year of the policy. The full financial effect of self-funding usually cannot be quantified until two or more years into the program.

At that point, the more expensive claims that occurred in the first year will begin to enter the final stages, as well as the smaller losses from the current and previous year that tend to settle in a shorter time span.

If you remember nothing else about self-insurance, make sure that you remember this: *when you buy traditional insurance, you are paying the claims up front, meaning that for the amount of premium you agree to pay, the insurance company will pay all covered claims for a specified period in the future.*

If you self-insure, you pay your claims yourself, and these claims are paid over time. Most property damage claims settle within the first 3 to 6 months, while higher-dollar bodily injury claims can take up to 5 years to settle, although most settle within 3 years.

The advantage of paying over time is that you can pay a claim that occurs today in the next three years, giving the company the use of the money as well as paying the loss at the value of the money three years in the future, which will be less than the value of those dollars today because of the use value and inflation. That's the good news.

The Bad News

The bad news is that you need to hire your own adjusting company (third party administrator—TPA) acceptable to the company insuring the next layer of insurance (excess carrier). It's your organization's responsibility for setting the oversight and authority requirements of the TPA.

This is still good news if your company dedicates resources to overseeing the program. This includes reporting claims, determining settlement authority limits, and funding the claims that are settled. A properly run self-insurance program can save your organization 30 percent in insurance costs or more!

OK, here's the actual bad news: once you begin self-insuring, your cash flow situation makes it very difficult to get out.

The reason for this is simple. Let's say your company loses its appetite for self-insurance after three years and wants to take advantage of a "soft market." You are hankering to get back to traditional, first-dollar coverage and its predictability. Your broker, in an attempt to pull you back into a more traditional (and more lucrative) program, will steer you toward this alternative.

If your company purchases a guaranteed cost policy, you are paying for future claims up front, and you will have to continue to fund all open claims from past years. Those claims will come due in the same policy period as the new guaranteed cost coverage, and because most large claims take time to settle, the dual cash outflows can and will lead to a cash flow nightmare. You will be paying the big claims from the self-insured period at the same time that you start paying the first dollar coverage (which funds all anticipated claims at the beginning of the policy period).

So, in a nutshell, if you get into a self-funding program and then decide to get back to traditional coverage, for a time you will be simultaneously paying for the past unpaid claims and the future claims.

The overlap will wash itself out over the next three to four years or so but will adversely and directly affect cash flow for at least two years after the company makes the switch back to a traditional program. Your organization, from the top down, needs to understand this before getting involved in a self-insurance program that is difficult to leave. Upper management needs to make the commitment from the beginning to help this program succeed. To do so, they need to know what the heck they are getting into. If an organization cannot sufficiently estimate its total claims costs one year into the future and if that company does not make a commitment to controlling these costs through safety or other risk-control measures, alternative risk-financing methods will not work.

At this point, it is valuable to distinguish between traditional insurance and alternative risk financing.

With traditional insurance, you are given a price for a specific period (policy period), usually a year, and you agree with the insurance company that this is the amount for the agreed coverage.

The payment for this coverage is generally financed with an initial deposit of 20 to 30 percent and 9 or 10 payments throughout the policy period.

- This may be done on the basis of a per-unit amount (auditable policy), such as per vehicle, gross revenues, payroll, and so forth, in which your costs are estimated at the beginning of the policy, and is audited by the insurer at a time after the policy has expired, or can be an agreement that the amount quoted is the agreed amount for certain coverage (flat policy).

- The insurance company agrees to pay all insured losses during that period, regardless of how many claims you have.

- Policies may have limits on the total amount that will be paid during the policy period (aggregate), but covered claims are generally paid as they occur.

- The price the insurer charges you is based on the estimated claims cost for that period, the expense the insurer expects to incur, and a reasonable amount for profit.

- If the department that prices the coverage (underwriting) collects more in premium than is paid in claims, all is well for the insurance company at the end of the day.

- If, overall, the insurer pays more in claims than they collect in premium, the insurer loses money on the policy, and you get the opportunity to work with a new underwriter next year.

- When the insurance company takes your premium money, they are not entitled to that money until the premium is actually used (earned premium). For example, if an insurer charges you a premium and takes the money up front, they cannot claim that premium as an asset until time passes and the policy is underway. In the simplest terms, if you have a one-year policy with a premium of $1,000, after six months you would have $500 in earned premium (an asset) and $500 as a liability (unearned premium). The insurance company can then take the earned premium and invest it to make more money.

In the United States, insurance regulators limit the type and amounts of premiums that can be invested so that insurers will have cash available or the opportunity to readily convert assets into cash to pay claims (liquidity). The insurance companies also have limits on the amount of insurance they can sell (capacity) to make sure that funds will be available to pay losses.

Insurers may only insure up to a certain amount (limit) to stay within its capacity limits, or they may go to another insurer and ask that carrier to insure the higher limits of the policy (reinsurance).

Reinsurance—It's Kind of Like Booking a Bet

Reinsurance works pretty much the same way as a bookie. Although I have never been to a bookie, I have always been amazed that bookies will take bets regardless of who you are betting on. They set odds on the chances of paying off, kind of like underwriting. The only difference is that they will take all bets, yet they never seem to take a bath.

Why, I always wondered. I figured one bad move and they'd been laid out somewhere. Well, a bookie who takes a large number of bets on one team will get to the point where he can't afford to risk the chance of losing and not being able to pay off. Therefore, when the capacity gets too big (too many folks bet on one team), he will call another bookie and bet a portion of the bets he has taken on the other team, thereby minimizing his winnings, but significantly reducing the chance of losses he cannot pay. Is this risk management? You bet.

Again, what you need to remember with traditional insurance is that you are paying all your claims up front. The insurance company comes in and evaluates your business, assets, loss history, and financial strength to see whether you are a good candidate to insure. If the insurer loses money on you, it will be because of claims activity, in which case your company will be paying a lot more for insurance when it comes time to renew the policy.

The reason that guaranteed cost insurance is the most popular form of insurance is because of its simplicity. It's pretty easy to understand: you pay the premium, they pay the claim. But it is also the most expensive because it is the riskiest kind of coverage for the insurance company. And because it is the riskiest for the insurer, it also creates the opportunity for the greatest return, which is why an insurer and their representatives (brokers and agents) will always steer your organization in the direction of traditional insurance.

There is an alternative, which is to become creative with the way that you manage your loss exposures (alternative risk financing).

Personal Alternative Risk Financing

You may not think of it this way, but you make risk-financing decisions in your personal life, and you make these decisions every day:

- If you own a vehicle, the state in which you reside requires that you carry a minimum amount of insurance on the vehicle in case you hit someone else (liability).

- If you finance your vehicle, you are probably required to carry collision and comprehensive insurance (physical damage coverage) on it. The financing company does this because if the vehicle suffers a major hit or is a total loss, you are less inclined to pay for a vehicle that doesn't work, and they need to be able to collect their money. That is why they name themselves on your policy (loss payee) and also register a lien on the title.

Almost all physical damage coverage comes with a clause that states that the insured (you) will determine an amount that you as the insured will pay before the insurer will start to pay (deductible). So, if you have a $250 deductible, you pay any claim up to that amount and the insurer pays the rest, up to the total value of the vehicle.

If you increase that amount to $1,000, it minimizes the insurer's risk because most physical damage losses are less than $1,000, and therefore the price for the coverage is lower. You should only do this, though, if you can financially handle the size of such a loss (tolerable risk).

If you get to the point where you don't need the coverage anymore (e.g., the vehicle is a piece of junk, the amount to insure it for physical damage exceeds the value of the vehicle), you may decide to drop the coverage altogether, knowing that the premium savings will need to be used to sustain or reduce a loss in the future.

This plan, going without insurance based on the belief that you can handle a loss when it occurs, is what we like to call self-insurance. Calling it self-insurance sounds better and makes people a little more comfortable than the traditional "no insurance" label.

Business Alternative Risk Financing

There are so many corporate alternative risk-financing techniques:

- You could become your own insurance company (captive insurer).

- You could get together with others whose businesses are similar (selfinsurance pools, risk retention groups).

- The three big ones you will get hit with are retro plans (retrospectively rated insurance plans), deductible plans, and SIR (self-insured retention) programs.

  The reason for this is simple: If you don't have a basic knowledge of these programs, you really have no business getting involved in any of the more complicated financing alternatives.

It is also valuable to determine how the company plans to fund the anticipated losses that will occur in the next 48 to 60 months:

- Most companies pay these claims when they come due (either through settlement or verdict) out of current cash flows (current expensing).

- Other companies will set up a spreadsheet that anticipates claims that will come due and the estimated amounts and will budget these amounts on a monthly or quarterly basis (unfunded reserves).

- Some companies will actually deposit funds into a dedicated account when a reserve is set and pay losses and expenses from this account (funded reserves).

While the most prudent funding technique is the funded reserve, most companies will generally pay losses through current expensing, which puts quite a bit of pressure on risk management and accounting to creatively buy enough time to get the cash together.

The reason for current expensing these claim payments is twofold:

1. Most companies are not disciplined enough to fund this account without a significant cash crisis causing an undue hardship on the entire organization.

2. Executives have a difficult time with cash sitting around in a funded reserve account, seemingly collecting dust in a short-term account, generating limited investment return.

The amount and liquidity of these funds make it very tempting for departments to attempt to convince the executive level that these funds would be more useful satisfying a department's short-term need.

Generally, the need for these funds are short-term, and because the money is presumed by members of the executive staff to be funds needed sometime in the future, they see no pressing need to repay the reserve fund.

Eventually, a department that taps into these funds will be unwilling or unable to replenish them, which will cause a firestorm of debate when the funds are needed to pay claims and they're just not there.

If the argument is convincing enough, these funds will be tapped, and once that cat is out of the bag, it's tough to develop a strong enough argument to refund the account, especially because every department will try to utilize this cash as a stopgap for a departmental shortfall.

Top-Down Commitment to Self-Funding of Claims

Should you decide that you are going to take advantage of the savings that alternative risk financing offers, you need to commit to managing the program, or it will wind up costing you more money, because you fund most of the claims.

If you are willing to invest the time and resources to manage these programs and you are also able to get a commitment to this type of program by the organization from the top down, you will save a lot of money, well in excess of the resources you commit.

A top-down commitment is necessary to ensure that the funds are made available when they are needed to pay claims. If a loss has been settled and all releases and agreements have been signed, the claim then becomes an obligation, and the check needs to go out immediately.

Retrospectively Rated Insurance Plans

Under retrospectively rated (retro) plans, there is an incentive for you to keep your claims as low as possible.

Under this plan, the insurance company charges a basic premium, and if your losses stay under certain thresholds after a predetermined period, you receive a premium rebate after the predetermined date.

For example, let's say you have a retro plan that costs $100,000 and the insurance company agrees to give you a 5 percent rebate if your losses are under 10 percent of the premium 12 months after the premium. If your losses are less than $10,000 after a year, you will get $5,000 back. This is a great deal…for the insurance company!

One thing is universal among all insurance companies: once they take your money, they don't like giving it back. Of course, they won't pay claims in order not to give you a rebate. But the insurer can structure the terms of the retro plan so they will have control of the plan, should they be inclined to find a need to oversee the numbers.

Claims are covered in depth in another chapter, but an overview is needed here.

When you look at a loss run, you will see that claims are broken down into these categories:

- Claims that have been paid already (paid claims).

- Amounts that the insurer estimates they will pay on that claim in the future (reserve).

- Paid and reserve are added together to give you the total amount of the claim (incurred).

- Expenses associated with that claim (allocated loss expense [ALE]).

With retro plans, as in traditional insurance setups, the insurer has control of the claims process. So, although there are techniques by which to delay a payment, the reserve is a rather subjective estimate of the amount the insurer will pay on that claim in the future. If your retro plan is based on incurred losses (which most are), the insurance company has the ability to estimate these claims.

I was actually in a situation in which my workers' compensation policy was set up as a retro plan based on incurred losses.

Two or three months prior to the anniversary dates, the reserves on the open claims would jump, and we would just miss the threshold to get the rebate. Culpability of the insurer is almost impossible to prove, and not all carriers do that sort of thing, although I can't say that for sure because that was my first and only retro plan.

If you do find yourself interested in a retro plan, ask that the rebate thresholds are based on paid losses rather than incurred losses. If the premium is significantly higher than for an incurred losses plan, reject both. Because the insurer does not have control over the loss history, they will generally charge a higher rate for the paid loss retro than they will for an incurred loss retro.

In an incurred retro plan, the insurance carrier has the ability to adjust the reserves to negate any rebate. The insurance carrier is like a baseball team that offers an incentive to a player if he plays in a certain number of games. If the season is drawing to a close and the team is out of contention but the player is ready to hit this "games played" incentive number, the organization may choose to sit the player down for the rest of the season to avoid paying the incentive. In baseball, it's called good business. In insurance, it's just plain wrong.

I'm not saying this will happen, but if your retro plan is based on incurred losses, you lose a lot of control over any return of premium. In a paid retro plan, the rebate is generally based on the insured staying below a percentage of paid claims on the predetermined future date. Since it is a percentage, the insurance company would be less inclined to pay a $10,000 claim to avoid paying a $5,000 premium return/rebate. You, the insured, help to keep the insurance company honest. They certainly will not pay more in one place to avoid paying less somewhere else.

The advantage of both programs is that the insurance company handles the claims and your organization doesn't have to mess with them. The disadvantage is that the insurance company handles the claims and you have no control whatsoever.

Deductible Programs

Deductible programs on liability policies are another good deal for the insurance companies, again from a control standpoint. In deductible programs, the insurance company handles and settles claims. When the claim is settled, the insurer will come back to you to fund the first portion of the loss.

As with retro plans, the advantage of deductible programs is that you don't have to deal with claims. The problems again come in when you do not understand the structure of the policy.

For example, let's say you have a deductible on your general liability policy in which your company pays the first $25,000 of each claim. Generally, a claim in excess of $10,000 or $15,000 will generate legal activity. If the other party (claimant) gets an attorney, the insurer will need to retain counsel, which will drive up the cost of the claim by 20 to 30 percent.

Now, if you were the insurance company, what would you do? Would you litigate a case that could end up costing a total of $50,000 for settlement and expenses, or would you offer $20,000 of someone else's money to make the problem go away?

The answer is so simple many companies fail to see it. If you give the insurer the ability to pay losses with your money, they are not going to be as frugal with it as they would with their own money, especially if the potential exists that the claim will get into their pocket. And if that's not enough, the inflated claim amount diminishes the strength of your loss history, and gives the insurer the rationale to raise rates in the future—because of claims they paid with your money!

Thus, a deductible program is a win all the way around for the insurance company. By contract, you are giving them the authority to settle any claim up to the maximum amount of the claim, and then they get to bill the deductible amount back to you.

And you sign up for this. You agree to this.

And the best part is the more they pay, the more they can charge you next year for this coverage. Therefore, there is no incentive to settle lower, as it will take more time and cost the insurer more. And the more they pay, the more the future premium goes up. All this with *your money*, and no added expense to the insurance company. What a deal.

Usually, the only occasion on which you will find an insurer aggressively fighting a deductible program claim is when the possibility exists that the claim will be settled in excess of the deductible. When the claim starts to affect their money, then they get infinitely more interested.

Self-Insured Retention (SIR) Programs

The major difference between self-insured retention programs and liability deductible programs is this:

- With deductible programs, the insurance company pays the entire claim, including the first portion your company has agreed to pay.

- In an SIR program, you pay the claims until you reach the agreed SIR threshold. For example, if you have a $1 million limit and a $100,000 retention limit per occurrence, your organization handles the claim until it reaches the amount that affects or touches the excess liability, and then the insurer takes over.

Some larger companies have the capacity to have their own claims department, although its structure and expertise level must be approved by the excess carrier.

Hiring an Adjusting Company

Most companies hire an adjusting company (third party administrator—TPA), which is an outside group that is licensed and contracted by you (the insured) to act on your behalf to settle losses you assign them.

Self-insured programs generally have reporting requirements once the incurred amount of the claim hits a percentage of the retention amount, usually between 25 and 50 percent of the retained limit. Using the example above, if the excess carrier requires the insured to start reporting the activities of a claim once its estimated value is more than 25 percent, the TPA would begin copying the excess insurer on all reports once the incurred loss amount (paid amount plus reserve) reaches $25,000. The reason for this is so the excess carrier can begin to gauge whether the case will exceed the self-insured amount and their layer of coverage is going to be affected. That's when they would need to get involved in the case (remember how they only become interested when there is a threat that the claim will go into their pocket).

Often, a TPA that handles the claim well will continue to handle it to settlement, especially those claims with the higher retention amounts.

The reason for this is twofold:

- *Continuity in defense of the claim.* It would not be wise to take the original adjuster and legal team off the case in the middle. The other side may perceive such a move as a sign of weakness. Replacing the legal and claims team that have been on the case from the beginning only extends the case. Given the fact that it could take years to settle anyway, it is not prudent to shift gears in the middle, although some insurers will choose to do so.

- ***Most excess carriers don't have strong claims departments.*** They provide coverage on high-SIR accounts because *they don't intend to pay any claims*. And they don't, with the exception of the most catastrophic losses. Excess carrier claims departments are geared to monitor the activities of the underlying SIR and are generally not prepared to handle the claim that exceeds (pierces) the SIR threshold and goes into the excess carrier's layer. They find it more cost effective to keep the current team in place and continue to monitor and direct the activities of the TPA and their continuing efforts.

For these reasons, if your company decides on an SIR, the success of the program depends on the strength of your choice of adjusting companies. I have found that there are two types of third party administrators:

- Those that do research into the circumstances of the claim to determine its relative value (processors).

- Companies that invest the time, effort, and resources to get the best settlement for the insured organization (investigative).

Processors simply get the claim in the office, gather cursory background information, and offer a settlement amount with little or no information gathered to allow them to properly value the claim. An investigative TPA, on the other hand, tends to treat your money like it's their own, and it does the groundwork necessary to mitigate and minimize a loss.

If you use a TPA that fights for every claim, you will find that your claim costs will rise, but the overall cost of your insurance program (cost of risk) will go down.

Investigative adjusting companies also appreciate, encourage, and solicit the assistance of the insured organization in the investigation of each claim, and it is in the insured's best interest to assist when they can, because this will minimize overall claims expenses.

I once had a broker call me and tell me that my TPA expenses were double the industry average. I told him that although this was true, my company's overall cost of insurance/risk was down over 20 percent. How could this be? What caused this to happen? I found it mildly amusing when I found out how he came to these numbers. It seems that claims costs are determined as a percentage of the total paid or incurred losses. In this particular industry, claims costs run about 15 percent of incurred losses. Our claims cost was over 30 percent.

What was happening, though, was that the TPA was so thorough and so prepared for each case that when it came time to sit down at the table and negotiate a settlement, all stones had been uncovered and the claimant and their representatives would come in with diminished expectations. Because the claim would usually settle lower than the actual value of the case and the costs were increased so this could be achieved in a great majority of the cases, the overall cost of the case would end up being lower.

Here's an example:

Let's say you have a loss that is reasonably valued at $50,000. During discovery and by utilizing intensive background work, it is discovered that the injury being claimed was actually preexisting. This information would not have been uncovered except for some expert investigation on the part of the adjuster, and the value of the claim without that information points to around $50,000.

With this information, the TPA is able to settle this case for $20,000 and $10,000 in claim costs. Thus, the total amount of the loss is $30,000. If the claim had been settled at the acceptable level, and this additional information had never been discovered, this claim would have cost the company $57,500 ($50,000 plus the 15 percent average, or $7,500).

Thus, the insured paid $10,000 (50 percent of the settlement) to reduce the amount from the accepted value of the claim to $20,000 and made a $50,000 claim go away in the process. The savings on this is $27,500 (52 percent) over the accepted estimate of the claim value, which is what your company would have been paid were it not for the commitment made to aggressively investigate all claims.

There is one way your company can get burned by this. If the TPA believes so strongly in its file, it may attempt to persuade you to take the case to court to defend it.

"We can win this thing!" they will tell you. They are looking for the slam dunk because, when the claim ends at the settlement table, it provides no additional income to the adjusting company. There is also some ego involved as well.

The knee-jerk reaction in our organization to the news of higher-than-average claims fees was to sharply curtail the activities of the TPA. I was able to prove that if we pay less to the TPA, we will pay more at settlement (which I had to approve), and shoot, if they did a really bad job, we could get that ratio down to 5 percent! The evidence that the overall cost of risk and insurance went down when the TPA came aboard bolstered the argument that aggressive management of claims will lower the overall cost of risk.

It is also valuable to define the procedure for paying and funding claims.

Some companies set up an escrow account that is funded at a tolerable financial level and into which the TPA can tap to pay approved claims. The escrow level is then replenished up to the agreed amount once the balance falls below a certain level.

It is very important to come to an agreement with your TPA as to their authority level in settling claims (drafting authority). If you have a large number of small claims, you may instruct the TPA that they have the authority to settle all claims with a dollar amount below $5,000. Any amount in excess of the agreed-upon value would have to be approved by the organization before a settlement is reached. If your organization has a small number of claims, you may require that the TPA seek approval on every case prior to settlement.

If you do not give the TPA authority to settle small claims, you will probably end up paying more for the administration of the claims process because the adjuster will have to prepare and provide to you the information necessary to make a settlement decision. The settlement-approval process also tends to lengthen the amount of time it takes to settle a case. This may adversely affect the small cases that have a very narrow window of opportunity to settle without counsel for either side. If the decision-making model requires the contracting company to bless every settlement decision, it may mean the difference between a reasonable settlement for very little cost and a claimant who gets frustrated, hires a lawyer, and continues the process while the value and the cost of the claim skyrocket.

I also understand that there is a transition period going from the insurer's claim department to a TPA, and trust needs to be established. It serves you and your organization to look at everything the TPA does and make clear that their authority to settle cases under a certain monetary threshold does not absolve them from oversight by the client they were hired to represent. Once trust is established, however, you should allow them to settle the smaller claims without the encumbrances of constant oversight.

If you have a high retention level, you will find that the majority of your claims will fall well below the retention amount, which makes you functionally self-insured. You are self-insuring the first layer, and the insurer comes in when your layer is exhausted. There is a difference, though, between being functionally self-insured and approved to be self-insured (qualified or statutory self-insurer). In this instance, state regulation requires you to register as a self-insurer and provide evidence that your organization has the financial strength to handle claims as they occur. Most states also require that a bond be posted. The need to qualify generally pertains to mandatory insurance such as auto and workers' compensation.

Structuring the SIR Is the Key

If you do decide on a self-insured retention program, make sure that your policy stipulates that allocated loss expenses are counted against your retention level.

Most large claims take years to settle. The main reason for this is the involvement of litigation in the process. Even if a claim is eventually settled out of court, there is much posturing prior to settlement. Let's use the $100,000 SIR limit again as an example. If the insuring agreement does not specify that allocated loss expenses (expenses that are paid to defend a particular claim) are counted against (erode) the retention level, and the loss exceeds $100,000, your contribution to that loss is $100,000, regardless of the amount it costs to defend the case.

If the insurance company agrees that allocated loss expenses do erode the SIR, and you have accrued $60,000 in costs to defend that action, your contribution becomes $40,000 because your loss expenses have reduced the SIR by $60,000. Failure to distinguish this in the insurance contract can lead to big surprises later on and can become a financial quagmire. It is also valuable to hammer out in detail what is considered an allocated loss expense ahead of time so the carrier does not try to nickel-and-dime your company, denying expenses using ambiguous language as its defense. The good news is that the insurance carrier will usually throw this erosion clause in for a nominal cost, especially if your claims rarely exceed the SIR.

You do need to be aware of the structure of the SIR to avoid big surprises.

The insurance contract will sometimes call for indemnity (claim payment) to be paid first, meaning that the amount for which the claim settles is funded first.

"No big deal," you say.

At first glance, it isn't. But check this out—let's say you have a $100,000 SIR and you have agreed to fund the claim first and then be reimbursed for your claims expense, which comes to $50,000. Now let's say the insurance company settles the claim for $200,000. Since you agreed to fund the settlement (indemnity) first, your portion of the indemnity is $100,000.

The agreement is to only reimburse for claim expenses that erode the SIR. Since the expenses do not erode the SIR in this instance because the claim amount was counted first, the insurer is not contractually obligated to reimburse these expenses. This is because once the claim goes into the insurer's level, the insurer pays the claim costs. Therefore, your total cost on this claim is $150,000 ($100,000 settlement plus the $50,000 loss expense).

So, although you have been paying out these expenses since the claim was first reported (in some cases between three and five years), because the settlement is funded first, your allocated loss expenses are written to erode the SIR and are not reimbursable once the SIR amount is hit.

If you are functionally self-insured, you may only have a claim that pierces the SIR level every two to three years. If you balk at the denial of claim costs, your insurance carrier will claim that you couldn't have been misled because you have had the same insurance arrangement for years!

Self-funding of claims can generate large savings for your company, but, as you can see, there are some huge considerations and even bigger potholes that need to be navigated before stepping into this arena. And once you get in, all levels of management need to understand that it is difficult to get out, especially if your company is dependent on consistent cash flow to ensure the continuity of operations.

If You Go Out, Stay Out!

In another life, I umpired baseball. When training for a three umpire rotation, we were taught that when the ball is hit in the gap, one of the three umpires needs to follow the ball into the outfield to determine whether a catch is made or whether the ball gets caught up in or rolls under the outfield fence. The rule on this play was, and I quote, "If you go out, stay out," meaning the other two umpires would cover all the other situations.

It's the same with self-insurance. Once you get into it, you need to stick with it to reap all the financial benefits. And if your organization has a true commitment to the program, and it also has the capability and resources to manage the program, the company will save significant cash in the long run.

That having been said, I was once the third base umpire in a championship youth league game. It was a big deal for a second-year umpire. The second batter hit a ball in the gap. I ran out and watched the outfielder pick the ball up, turn, and throw it to the cutoff man, who was in short left field. I started moseying back to the infield, knowing that the first base ump would cover first and second and the home plate umpire would make any calls at third and home.

As I started back, I saw the batter round second and head to third. I first looked to third and then through third to see the plate umpire standing behind home plate with his thumb up his...well, let's just say he wasn't paying attention.

I ran in as fast as I could but ended up making a call on a bang-bang (close) play from about 150 feet away. Although this was a short-term problem, and even though it happened in the top of the first inning, it did not cause me to deviate from the plan. I tore into the plate umpire. Boy was he moving the rest of that game. In fact, in every subsequent three-man-crew situation, I made sure that the "if you go out" rule was spelled out before the game to ensure a similar problem wouldn't happen again. Now, that's what I call risk management.

Familiar Ground

There are no hard-and-fast rules for your insurance program, but when you make a significant move (like the one to self-insurance), be prepared for all possible ramifications. The inability to adapt and improvise will cost you money.

Self-insurance can generate real cost savings to an organization that is willing to commit to it. Although there are significant savings, especially in the first year, there are also start-up and operational costs involved in handling claims on your own. Failure to have a top-down understanding of the risks and benefits will leave the executive level of your company doubting the wisdom of such a program, and, without this commitment, the program is doomed to failure.

I once worked at a company that had a wildly successful self-insurance program for all the aforementioned reasons. It was so successful, in fact, that the company decided to get into a self-funding arrangement with its health insurance carrier. Health insurance, because it was a company benefit, was handled by the human resources/payroll department, not the risk-management department.

At the end of the first three quarters, the costs of the self-funded health insurance stood at 110 percent of the premium allocated. The HR department tried to mitigate losses by pursuing subrogation claims from employees who may have been compensated from another source, such as in tort liability or workers' compensation cases.

Let me tell you something; employees don't like to be questioned about such matters, and the companies are actually precluded from doing this by law. Needless to say, we were back into a guaranteed cost arrangement the next year. Was this because it was more cost effective to do so? We'll never know. The organization decided they didn't have the stomach for self-funded health insurance and decided to cut their losses and get back onto familiar ground.

If your company is more comfortable on familiar ground, a self-funding arrangement may not be for you either. But if your organization has an appetite for risk, a history of success in its risk taking, and the willingness to commit to the chosen program, there is a lot of cash to be saved.

Let me say that again.

There Is a Lot of Cash...

8

The Power of Positive Audit Experiences

What You Don't Know about the Audit Process Can Hurt You

I remember the first audit I had. I worked for a car rental company, and the insurance company needed to send someone to count the number of days our car rental vehicles were out on rent. Our premium was calculated by the number of rental days the cars were actually out because we felt that this number most accurately represented the company's exposure.

In the past, the premium had been determined as a percentage of total revenue. This total was very easy to track and to validate. The problem I had with this approach is that it did not accurately represent our exposure.

If you have ever rented a car, then you know that the price of a rental vehicle differs depending on where and why you rent the vehicle. If you rent a vehicle at an airport location, it will cost significantly more than if you rent from a suburban outlet, even if it's from the same company. Also, if you rent a car on the weekend at the airport, it will cost less than it does during the week.

Car rental prices are tied to supply and demand. Most car rental companies actually have entire departments to survey, track, and verify the rates of competitors and then adjust their prices accordingly.

Counting rental days takes the price variance out of the calculation for actual exposure. Thus, we were able to get a company to quote us on a rental day basis. This was a new concept at the time, and I'm not sure the insurance carrier had thought the whole thing through to the auditing of the information reported.

We would agree to an initial premium and pay it over the policy period. We would then have an auditor come in and validate the actual number of days after the end of the policy period and multiply the number of rental days by the rate.

If that number was in excess of the premium deposit we paid at the beginning of the contract, the company owed money. If it was less than that, we would get a refund.

I got the notice for this first auto policy audit from an independent auditing firm about 45 days after the policy period ended.

The first thing that set me off was the fact that I couldn't even determine whether this auditor was male or female. The letter was signed by an ambiguous and nondescript "B. Smith." I imagined some awful creature living in the basement of the insurance building, only venturing out when it was time for another—*audit!*

B. Smith had to have been one such animal. Someone opened up the cellar door and stirred B. Smith with a long stick before sedating, transporting, and releasing the creature in the lobby of my office building.

So I did what any good insurance professional would do when faced with the unknown—*I threw the letter away.*

That strategy worked so well that I threw the second letter away as well…and the third.

The fourth one bummed me out. With the other letters, there was no real proof that the company had received it. This one came in the form of the ever ominous certified letter with return receipt requested.

There were only two reasons why I didn't discard this letter:

1. I don't know about your office, but whenever a certified letter with return receipt requested came to me, the whole office wanted to know what was in it. Sometimes, someone would open it, see what it was, and then apologize to me for opening it. I would then tell everyone eavesdropping on the conversation that it was probably a garnishment notice for unpaid child support. That would miraculously cause half of them to disappear immediately.

2. The insurer sent it certified with return receipt requested so they would know that I received it, thus eliminating the premise for my one and only excuse.

An Auditor's Ultimate Goal

So, four months later came the big audit day, when I would finally meet B. Smith (if that was his or her real name).

Well, in walked Bob Smith, a little disheveled yet not really annoyed that it took him four months to get in. I had no idea how he was going to measure this rental day premium basis thing. Apparently, neither did he.

I had my little four-page report in my hand. I told him that we had approximately 900,000 rental days, and with the average length of rental being 3.5 days, it came to, oh—approximately 257,143 contracts to audit. The good news, I told him, was that all the contracts were right there on the premises.

Bob Smith began to shiver and twitch, apparently in a vain attempt to remember where on his body he had hidden the cyanide capsule. OK, he wanted to know, what was the other alternative? I wanted to tell him there was no other way, but at this point he was on the verge of tears.

I told him I had this comprehensive four-page report that quantified all the information in that storeroom. I handed him a copy of the report.

He dabbed his eyes with a tissue and rather sheepishly asked, "Do you mind if I take this and convert it into my own spreadsheet?"

"Sure," I replied, "as long as you don't offer to take me to lunch!"

Apparently the thought of having lunch with me was as appealing to him as it was to me, so that was it. I gave him my business card and Bob Smith gave me his, had me sign the release or whatever it is he had me sign, and shuffled off into the sunset. He had arrived at about 10:15 AM. He was gone before noon.

Bob Smith taught me a valuable lesson that day. When I share this lesson with people, I like to ask this question:

What is an insurance auditor's primary objective?

These are the answers I get:

- To validate that the insured has actually paid in premium what they agreed to

- To make my life miserable

- To generate more income for the insurance carrier

- To get an overall feel for the insured's operations

Wrong, wrong, wrong, and wrong! Now, these are objectives of some auditors, but none of them is the primary objective, as Bob Smith taught me. I learned that the auditor's objective does not change regardless of the breadth of work involved in the audit process, the time it took to travel, or how lost he got trying to find the place.

It really doesn't matter whether it's an in-house auditor or an independent auditor. The primary objective of an auditor is *to get home by noon!*

The Results Are in the Preparation

The point of this is not to take advantage of this knowledge to pull a fast one over the insurance carrier. That would be wrong.

I am saying, however, that if all the information is forwarded to the auditor in a comprehensive package with a tie-in report that validates those numbers, and the corresponding paperwork is there to back it up, you have done 90 percent of the auditor's work. The auditor is then free to do as he or she pleases.

An independent auditor is generally paid by the audit, so the amount of work is irrelevant to the carrier, but it frees up that person's time to do more audits... or go fishing.

If it's a company (in-house) auditor you're dealing with, know that his supervisor will give him a time limit to complete the audit. If that time limit is 2 days and he is out of your office in 45 minutes, he's got some unstructured time coming.

Let's look at it another way. Suppose the auditor comes in and you give him a banker's box filled with W-2s and a handwritten cash receipt register, and the audit takes four days to complete. He tries to find you, but you're cowering in the bathroom. That auditor is going to draw his own conclusions. And if you make the auditor jump through those hoops, he is going to find something to charge you additional for. Wouldn't you?

If you were an auditor, and it took you twice as long to do an audit as your time estimate, I can guarantee one thing—you would find something to charge against the policy for all that work. And you would also be less inclined to entertain any valid claims you might have to any misclassified premium or other discrepancies.

Which auditor will generally be more receptive to your organization and more apt to give you the benefit of the doubt? Who will be more receptive to your interpretation of manual rates classification of employees and excluded expense bases as well as the treatment of loss exposures? Why, Bob Smith, of course.

Workers' Compensation Audits

The biggest cost in work comp policies and the ensuing audits is due to the misclassification of employees' payroll. The common mistake that most companies make in respect to this is when they give the auditor the employee's title, which may or may not correspond to his or her duties.

For example, you may have a manager who travels from office to office or job site to job site. If you call him a supervisor, the insurance company could recognize him as a foreman, which by definition gives that person direct supervisory authority over the workers at that site and would put him in the same classification as the direct workers.

Let's use another common example: you have a very large sales staff that is supported by a rather large administrative staff. If you put the word *sales* into their titles, more often than not, this payroll will be placed in the sales classification, even though these are clerical employees who handle the administrative functions for the sales department. The difference here is only about 1/2 percent, but if you have an administrative staff with payroll of about $1 million, proper classification yields a savings of about $5,000—without really trying.

These classification errors are generally not picked up by companies, and correcting them will generate little discussion and no argument from the auditor. Auditors generally will not offer to reclassify your employees to a less expensive class.

Leveling the Playing Field

In the Scopes manual, which defines the scope of work each employee should be classified for work comp premium pricing, there are gray areas that can be argued both in the more expensive category by the insurer and the less expensive category by you, the employer or insured. I caution you, though, to classify only that payroll for which you can actually provide a defensible argument. If you do consider an employee to have been misclassified, place that payroll in the more financially advantageous class, which forces the insurer to justify placing that employee in a more expensive classification.

The burden of proof is on the insurance company to validate their argument for reclassifying, instead of on you to justify why the employee or employees should be moved to a cheaper classification.

As for the preparing the audit package in anticipation of the audit, here are some tips to make the auditor's life (and yours) a lot easier:

- If your policy does not renew on January 1, use the previous calendar year as a proxy for audit purposes. That will give the auditor the opportunity to tie in the payroll with the quarterly tax statements while still giving an accurate snapshot of your company's payrolls. For this to be valid, it's best to have your renewal in the first quarter, with the best policy renewal window occurring between February 1 and March 15.

This gives you the opportunity to gather the calendar year paperwork that will tie the numbers in for the auditor. Remember, your numbers need to tie in with the numbers that are on the tax statements and the payroll reports. Tying them in to the previous calendar year as a proxy allows the auditor to verify and balance the two sources.

If Your Renewal Date Is January 1, Move It!

- The end of the calendar year is the busiest time of the year for the insurance industry, and while all the numbers will match up on audit, your organization may not get the attention it deserves from underwriters on renewal. You will find yourself going into the eleventh hour to renew your policy (which by the way is New Year's Eve), and more often than not, you will end up signing for a program you are not satisfied with, only because you ran out of time.

- Contact your payroll company or department and ask them to contour payroll reports. They will be able to break out each individual payroll into separate categories such as overtime, meals, per diem, travel, cell phone, and so forth.

- When you provide the auditor with a certified report that ties into the tax records, it eliminates the need to pore over vast mounds of W-2s, which eliminates at least two minutes per employee. If you have one hundred employees, that's three and a half hours saved. If you have five hundred employees, it will save the auditor an entire day.

- Educate yourself about those portions of payroll that are to be excluded. By definition, there are items that show up as income that may be excluded under NCCI rules. Generally, bonuses, incentive pay, universal leave, housing, and training are included as payroll.

- Overtime is included, but is calculated at a discounted rate because the amount of overtime needs to reflect the increased pay amount for the same exposure. Most auditors will calculate overtime as time and a half. If you have substantial payroll that is paid in excess of time and a half (e.g., holiday pay, weekends), you need to bring this to the attention of the auditor. Be prepared to substantiate overtime in advance of the day of the audit. If your overtime is entirely or substantially paid at time and a half, overtime is reduced by one third, or by dividing the entire overtime amount by 1.5. Per diem, expense reimbursement, auto allowance, and cell phone are examples of income that is generally excluded from payroll. Breaking the payroll out by category allows you to quantify this for the auditor. Generating the quarterly payroll reports gives you the opportunity to foresee your costs throughout the year instead of being surprised when the audit occurs.

If the insurance auditors are left to their own devices, they will generally plug employees into the more expensive class even if they fit nicely into the less expensive classification. Your goal is to ensure that all employees are properly classified and that their income is properly slotted in accordance with the rules, regulations, and guidelines put forth by both state regulation and NCCI.

There are conflicting forces at work here. The insurer will place employees into the more expensive class because it's difficult to argue them up from a less expensive class. Likewise, if you place your employees in the higher (more expensive) class, you have little argument to putting them into a less expensive classification after the audit is completed. These strategies will even the playing field, and isn't that all you're asking for anyway.

General Liability Audits

General liability (GL) policies are most often based on gross revenues or payroll. Payroll is typically only the direct employees (those actually producing the product or delivering the service) and their supervisors.

The most important thing to understand in GL polices is that most of them will require a minimum premium, which means that if the premium upon audit is calculated to be higher than the initial premium, your company pays the difference. If the premium is less than the minimum or initial premium, you get nothing.

For this reason, it is essential that you conservatively estimate your payrolls prior to executing the general liability policy. The insurance companies know this, and thus will usually not compel you to report a formula or a historically based payroll number. Therefore, regardless of how you like to fund your insurance policies, it's always better to pay a little more upon audit than not get anything back because you overestimated the payrolls.

How do I know? Don't ask.

Suffice it to say that my ability to overlook this aspect of the policy caused some consternation at one time during my career. My loss is your gain.

General liability policies, as with most commercial policies, require a minimum on the policy to ensure the policy is not cancelled shortly after inception. This could be as much as 35 percent, which your company would have to pay even if the policy was cancelled the day after it was written.

Automobile Audits

Auto insurance is based on the number of vehicles times the base rate of the class of vehicle (e.g., passenger vehicle, light truck, heavy-duty vehicle). On a scheduled policy (each vehicle is covered if it is named or "scheduled" on the policy, similar to your personal auto policy form), you pay the premium when you add the vehicle, and this type of policy is not subject to audit. With a composite auto policy, you are generally charged for the amount of time the vehicle is on the policy, and you pay a flat rate for each vehicle for each class.

With composite policies, you need to read the policy to see how the premium is going to be calculated upon audit. If the premium is calculated by each month the vehicle is in service, you will pay for a whole month even if you acquire that vehicle on the last day of that month.

These savings will only be of consequence if you are frequently acquiring and disposing vehicles.

The Significance of Audit Planning

Now, let me tie this up into a tight little audit package.

The reason I was so afraid of the auditor, B. Smith, was not because of what he or she might do to me. I was afraid because of what I had done to myself. I was not in a position to determine what the eventual premium would be, and therefore, I could not prepare upper management as to what might be the result of this audit.

Because of my inattention and lack of planning, I had no idea what to expect from the auditor. I didn't even know what was going to be audited.

There is a big hint here: if you are unable to figure out how the premium basis will be audited efficiently by the insurance company, chances are they won't know either. All would be well if there is a refund, but all heck would break loose if the company owes the insurer an amount that would affect cash flow, even in the short run.

In short, prepare for the audit—not when the policy expires, but all throughout the policy period. Have an adequate estimate of how your premium basis will affect the premium. Be able to answer critical questions. If payroll goes up, how high will the work comp premiums go? If gross revenue increases 20 percent, how does that impact the GL? Your boss may know that business is booming and that insurance costs will increase because of this, but he or she needs to be prepared for the specific ramifications and how they result in additional premium.

The Appeal Process

One last thing—I almost always appeal my company's audits. The reason? The number one reason is because the auditor made a mistake or two. The other reason, though, is to buy some time to pay any additional premium that becomes due upon audit.

If the audited (previous) policy and the current policy are with the same carrier, an assessment on the previous policy will usually become due immediately, and failure to pay will result in the cancellation of the existing policy. Simply put, if you don't pay the audited amount immediately, the insurance carrier may cancel the existing policy, especially if it's an extension of the previous year's policy.

The best way to figure out whether the two policies are related is to see whether the policy number or account number is the same on both. The insurer will use this as a hedge to compel you to pay the audit amount. This is really not fair, but it is a reality. Appealing the audit will usually buy you three to six months to get the corrections made and figure out how to pay the balance.

Managing the audit process is essential to managing your costs. If you establish precedents within a policy governing classifications, income evaluation, or qualifying income, and you are aware of which aspects of the process are etched in stone and which aspects are subject to interpretation, not only will you be able to significantly reduce your costs, you will also have the ability to predict the premium costs into the next policy period and beyond with a high degree of accuracy.

Level the Playing Field by Learning the Game

PART II
Understanding Your Insurance Policies

Part 2 is all about insurance policies. To effectively use the strategies outlined in Part 1, it is essential that you understand what each policy covers. Although you may find commercial insurance polices confusing, there is actually a structure to them that is similar in each line of insurance.

This section explains the structure and educates you on where in the policy you can find the information you need:

- What is covered and what is not

- Who is covered

- The time period (policy period) that the insurance covers

- Who is considered an insured and who isn't

The following part of the text is intended to show you how to read your insurance policy. It is not intended to supplant the expertise of your insurance advisors or to act as a catchall for insurance knowledge, and it is not intended to be a comprehensive and exhaustive analysis of your insurance policies or programs.

Instead, I will show you what to look for in each policy and help you determine at a glance whether you have adequately insured your organization's exposures.

Then you will be able to determine whether you are receiving what you think you are paying for in each policy.

Face it—you're going to have to read the policies.

The following chapters concentrate on traditional guaranteed cost programs. These policies can apply to self-insuring options as well because most alternative risk-financing policies are written on a standard insurance contract with the self-funding terms provided by endorsement or referred to in a separate insuring agreement.

9
Insurance 101—Automobile Liability

Your Company's Single Most Important Risk

Auto liability is the single most important form of coverage you will need in your business, period. Converging forces in your daily operations can lead to disaster, and if you don't have the proper insurance in place when this disaster arrives, your liability could bankrupt your company faster than any other event.

Let's break it down:

- You are entrusting a 2,000-plus-pound piece of equipment to an employee, who you may or may not have qualified as a driver by checking his driving history.

- This employee needs to move this vehicle from place to place to perform his or her assigned duties; there is really no business I know that does not need transportation at some point to deliver its products and/or services.

- It is difficult to determine what the employee does and where the employee goes once he or she leaves the lot. Once the driver leaves your premises, there is not a lot you can do to stop that employee should they choose to go wherever folks go when they're supposed to be working.

- These vehicles have lots of power.

- There are whole bunches of other people running around in similar vehicles, as well as in vehicles that may be bigger and more powerful.

- These other vehicles may or may not follow the traffic rules and may run into your vehicle. Despite your best preparations, it is very difficult to protect an employee if he or she happens upon a situation in which another vehicle, animal, or other road hazard causes a loss to occur.

It's All about Control (or Lack Thereof)

The one theme that runs through this exposure is control. Once the vehicle leaves your sight, there is really no opportunity to control the actions of your driver. More important, you are unable to control the actions of others on the road, and it is these variables that eventually lead to a loss, either through the fault of your driver or the fault of another.

The following questions, when answered, lead to the variables of employee transportation over which you have a degree of control:

- Will my driver follow the rules of the road?

- Is my driver physically able to perform the task?

- Have I placed responsibilities and deadlines on a driver that may cause him to choose to meet the deadline over driving safely?

- If the vehicle is in an accident and is disabled for a time, does the company have a cost-effective replacement vehicle source so that the accident will cause little interruption of daily operations?

It is inherently difficult to survive in the business world without transportation, and the cost of outsourcing transportation is just not realistic. There are many ways in which to reduce the cost of automobile liability:

- Use general risk-reduction principles.

- Use a little bit of common sense.

- Prepare for the eventuality of an auto loss and have a plan in place.

Types of Commercial Auto Policies

There are two basic types of auto coverage.

In the first type, you name each auto on the policy and pay for any additional coverage on a per-vehicle basis (scheduled auto policy). In essence, your vehicle is named on the policy's schedule. If the vehicle is named, you, as the owner, are insured by that policy.

A scheduled auto policy mirrors the type of policy you have on your personal vehicles. The vehicles are only covered if the vehicle is named on the policy. The premium is paid when the vehicle is added and is credited when the vehicle is dropped.

The advantage to a scheduled policy is that you can pick and choose which vehicles will carry additional coverage such as physical damage, towing, and so forth. The disadvantage is that as your fleet grows, it becomes increasingly difficult to manage the coverage. There will always be a trade-off between management oversight and cost. This is true in all aspects of business. Realizing significant savings requires your company to become more actively involved in all aspects of the insurance and risk-management program.

The other type of fleet liability insures all fleet vehicles equally, meaning that as vehicles are added, they have the same coverage as every other vehicle in the fleet (composite auto policy).

On a composite policy, the insurer figures out the total value of your fleet and computes a premium based on the average price per vehicle. The insurer then adds in all the coverage you want on each vehicle and assesses a rate on a per-vehicle basis. This means that all vehicles in the fleet are assessed the same annual premium.

The insurer generally will break the coverage into separate vehicle categories, such as personal passenger vehicles (PPVs), light trucks, and trucks. As vehicles are added and deleted from the policy, they are assessed the agreed premium for the type of vehicle under which it is classified and the premium is assessed pro rata.

The formula for calculating the pro rata basis of vehicles should be in your composite auto policy. Some policies will assess added and deleted vehicles differently, which could cost you or save you additional premium. This premium would not be significant unless you add or delete a lot of vehicles during the policy period.

For example, some policies prorate monthly. Under these policies, the insured is charged for a vehicle that is acquired or sold at any time during a particular month, even if the vehicle only touches that month for one day. Other policies use the fifteenth of each month to determine whether that month should be included. If a vehicle is added prior to the fifteenth, the insured is not assessed for that month. If the same vehicle is added after the fifteenth, the insured is charged for the entire month. Still other policies divide the premium by the actual number of days in the policy and then multiply this by the number of days the vehicle is in the fleet during the policy period.

Although the daily assessment is the most equitable to you as the insured, it is also the most confusing and leads to the most errors upon audit. It also requires the most documentation.

The major advantage of the composite policy is its simplicity. It is pretty straightforward, and, as auditable policies go, it is generally the easiest to calculate.

If you have to figure out a daily rate to determine your insurance costs, it defeats one of the major attractions of the policy.

If you are going to manage the fleet, then the daily assessment may be the way to go from an insurance standpoint. Your head will explode, though, trying to figure out the audited numbers. Hey, maybe that's the insurer's goal.

Auto Liability Coverage Explained

The limits of the policy are important as well. Have you ever asked your broker what your liability limits are, and he says 100, 300, and 50? You figure you're supposed to know this, so you don't ask more questions. You're just glad to get off the phone so quickly.

If your policy carries 100/300/50, it basically tells you the maximum amounts the insurer will pay per occurrence, multiplied by $1,000:

- The first number (100) is the maximum amount per thousand (or $100,000) the policy will pay out to any one person for bodily injury in an accident that is your fault.

- The second number (300) is the maximum amount the policy will pay out ($300,000) for any one accident.

- The third number (50) is the maximum amount the policy will pay for property damaged due to your negligence ($50,000).

Sometimes, you will see a single number followed by the letters *CSL*. This number is the maximum amount that will be paid under the policy for any one occurrence. So if you have a policy that reads $1,000,000 CSL, it means that there is a combined single limit of $1 million. It does not have per person or property limitations.

Liability insurance is mandatory in all but five states: Tennessee, New Hampshire, Wisconsin, South Carolina, and Virginia. Each of these states does have requirements to validate your financial responsibility, either by paying into an uninsured motorist fund or proving you are financially able to be uninsured (or, as some would say, self-insured).

All automobile policies, regardless of whether they are composite or scheduled policies, have certain additional coverage that can be elected and added:

- ***Collision coverage***—physical damage from a collision regardless of fault. You wreck your vehicle, collision pays…less your deductible. The higher the deductible, the lower the cost of collision.

- *Comprehensive (comp) coverage*—physical damage from all other damage that occurs beyond your control, such as wind, hail, flood, fire, and so forth. If the car gets wrecked through no fault of your own, comp covers. Basically, it covers most losses that are not collision losses.

- *Towing*—reimburses up to a certain amount in the event your vehicle needs to be towed. Some policies afford this only due to an incident or accident that causes the vehicle to become disabled and do not cover towing for mechanical breakdown.

- *Personal Injury Protection (PIP)*—medical payments that supplement liability coverage. PIP is mandatory in some states and is generally extended regardless of fault.

- *Drive other vehicle coverage*—This extends coverage to named drivers who may not have personal auto coverage and who drive other vehicles. This endorsement is valuable for executives who drive a company car yet do not own their own vehicle and may be occasioned to drive another person's vehicle. For example, you may be an executive who has negotiated the use of two vehicles, one for you and one for your wife. In the event you need personal coverage on a vehicle you or she drives that is not a company vehicle, this provision provides that coverage. The driver needs to be named on the auto policy on the drive other vehicle endorsement. Drive other vehicle coverage follows the named driver and not the vehicle.

- *Rental car versus rental reimbursement coverage*—Rental car coverage covers you and your employees when you rent a car while traveling on business. Rental reimbursement is the amount the policy will pay to reimburse for the cost of renting a vehicle while your vehicle is in the shop due to a covered event or loss. Rental reimbursement coverage will usually have a per-day limit as well as a time limit, such as $30 per day up to a maximum of $900. Some insurers will agree to pay for a more expensive vehicle for a shorter period. This is the exception, though, so discuss this before you go out and rent that stretch limo. The insurer *will not* pay more than the maximum amount allowable on the policy for this coverage. It is also important to note that your credit card may provide coverage for an employee while on travel, although many business credit card accounts will require enrollment as well as a fee for this service. You can get coverage for vehicles rented or borrowed by company employees on company business as an add-on (rider) on the scheduled policy. This will preclude the company from having to pay those outrageous car rental insurance fees, which no one needs (unless, of course, you don't have the coverage elsewhere).

- ***Uninsured Motorist (UM) coverage***—extends coverage if a fleet vehicle is involved in an accident with an uninsured vehicle. This coverage is mandatory in some states. In these instances, UM coverage is extended through the liability aspect of the policy and replaces the coverage the uninsured motorist should have had. UM will cover the bodily injuries to the driver and passengers in your vehicle as well as the damage to your vehicle in most states, regardless of deductible or whether you have physical damage coverage at all! I advise that you elect this coverage even if it's not mandatory in your state.

  Eighteen states require uninsured motorist coverage for vehicles registered in that state. Don't worry, though. If it's mandatory, you already have it and you just don't know it, which also means that you paid for it and didn't know about it either.

It is important to note that all these coverages are available on both the scheduled and composite policies. The composite policy will add all coverage elected to all vehicles, while with the scheduled policy you can pick and choose particular coverages for individual vehicles. Most companies, though, tend to have one or the other.

If it is the scheduled policy, coverage is generally tailored to the most expensive vehicles. If the scheduled policy is not monitored and managed, you may end up with a fully insured pickup truck worth less than the annual physical damage premium you are paying.

The scheduled policy allows you to choose to insure the more expensive vehicles for physical damage and allows you to drop coverage on vehicles for which the premium exceeds the value of the vehicle. The composite policy does not have this flexibility, which is why most companies tend to gravitate toward scheduled auto coverage. As I stated before, though, your organization may find itself overinsuring some vehicles and underinsuring others if the fleet isn't effectively managed. On the other hand, a composite policy on a diverse fleet will almost ensure that some vehicles will have too much insurance while others will not have enough.

Why Not Use the Scheduled and Composite Policies Together?

My solution: buy both policies. Determine the current value of each vehicle, and pick a number your organization can live with if there were a total loss, such as a value (actual cash value) of $10,000.

Place all vehicles that have a value over the actual cash value (ACV) threshold on the scheduled policy with full coverage. Place all those below that threshold on a composite policy with very little additional coverage (bare-bones policy). As a result, the $100,000 Mercedes, which would cause a cash flow nightmare if it were totaled, would be fully insured. The ten-year-old pickup truck worth $2,000, however, would not be insured for physical damage.

What If the Bank Holds the Note?

You generally need physical damage coverage to satisfy the bank that is financing the vehicle. You cannot be uninsured, but you can be "self-insured." It's really all in the way you present it.

You can break up your coverage any way you want. You can choose to cover the sales and executive vehicles and use the composite policy for work and field vehicles. The company would load all the additional coverage onto the schedule policy and insure the work fleet vehicles at an acceptable level of liability on the composite policy.

Each year upon renewal, review your needs and adjust the ACV threshold up or down as necessary. Next, value those vehicles that are currently on the scheduled policy. If the value has dropped below the threshold, delete it from the scheduled policy and add it to the composite policy.

Driver Approval

Most insurance carriers will give steep discounts if you agree to qualify your drivers and have them approved by the insurance carrier before they are allowed to drive a company vehicle. The insurance company will give you minimum requirements for these drivers, such as two or fewer minor tickets in three years, or one major in two years.

It is extremely valuable to qualify all drivers prior to hiring them, by verifying their driving history as well as their criminal history. You don't want to hire someone who has a great driving record but a history of car theft. You also do not want to hire a criminal with a great driving record and a bent toward fencing stolen goods.

If your organization is not presently qualifying its drivers, you should start immediately. Note: It is required by the Fair Credit Reporting Act that each employee is notified and agrees in writing to allow your company to check his or her driving record and criminal history. Once you enact this policy, you should have all current drivers sign the disclosure form and then check their records semiannually. Once you begin screening drivers, you will see a dramatic decrease in the number of accidents and losses your company experiences. When you are able to decrease the number of accidents, you statistically reduce the big losses as well. This improves your loss history. Minimizing both the frequency (number) and severity (amount) of your losses leads to a reduction in premium.

Using the Drug-Free Workplace to Qualify the Drivers

It is also valuable to institute a drug-free workplace (DFWP). Doing so enhances the candidate-qualification process and leads to a significant reduction in losses.

Drug testing, as long as it is comprehensive (including a program for random, post-accident, and reasonable suspicion testing as well as counseling) is not discriminatory and has been upheld by the courts as a valid qualifier for employment.

Companies can also legally adopt a zero-tolerance policy in which any employee can be terminated upon receipt of a positive drug test result. Instead of termination, a company can also offer rehabilitation to employees who test positive in a random, post-accident, or reasonable suspicion test. Whichever way the company chooses to handle positive test results, it must be comprehensive and consistent to avoid discrimination.

To avoid any surprises later, it's best to require potential employees who are interviewing for driver jobs or who may drive to bring a current copy of their driving record when they apply for the position. If you make this a requirement before the applicant can get an interview, it will save the company a great deal of time in the hiring process by weeding out those who don't qualify before the interviews start.

In fact, most folks who know they won't pass either the drug testing or the minimum requirements to drive will usually not bother to apply, which saves a lot of time in the initial stages of recruiting.

The Named Driver Policy

Another unique auto policy worth mentioning may be useful when your organization has a large fleet of vehicles and a smaller pool of drivers who have access to them. In such an instance, instead of scheduling the vehicles, the company schedules the drivers, who are then covered in any vehicle owned by the company (named driver auto policy).

I was able to use this as backup coverage in the car rental industry so that managers who had 24-hour access to vehicles as part of their compensation would have additional coverage in case of a catastrophic loss that could adversely affect the primary fleet policy. This avoided the need to assign vehicles to specific employees, rendering the vehicle ineligible to generate income while assigned to that employee. This also kept many employee losses off the primary insurance policy.

The major drawback of the named driver policy is that the coverage will not fulfill the minimum liability requirements of each vehicle since the coverage follows the driver and not the vehicle.

The rule of thumb is this:

- Insure for the losses that would adversely affect the company financially (bodily injury liability loss exposures).

- Self-insure for those hits you can take (physical damage on lower-priced vehicles).

Small one-car accidents or losses that occur in a parking lot while unattended should generally be handled outside of insurance. Refer bodily injury claims to your carrier or third party administrator. You never know when a bodily injury claim will take on a life of its own, even in instances in which the injury appears to be minor. Take care of the losses you can pay for, insure for the losses you can't handle…

And pocket the difference.

10
Insurance 101 — Property/ Package Coverage

Why Do I Have to Insure Packages?

Sometimes, you will find coverage that is seemingly so straightforward that you figure no one could possibly find a way to make it extraordinarily complicated.

You might think, for example, that a building should be covered for its value and when a flood or fire comes along and totals the thing out, you should be covered. You might also assume you could insure any special risks as well as the individuals who are on the property for business-related purposes.

You couldn't be more wrong.

Property coverage is so straightforward that in order to ensure that you are totally confused by it, the insurance industry has created what it calls a package policy into which they have bundled a whole bunch of different products. Ostensibly, the intent of this was to roll smaller but related policies into one consolidated policy (e.g., package them all together). So they put all this stuff in there so when it's time to read the policy or you have a loss and need to see whether it's covered, you have no idea where to look and what to look for.

By the time you are done reading it, I guarantee you your head will explode. And if, for some unknown reason, your head doesn't explode and somehow your sanity remains intact, this property policy will hit you with that formula designed to ensure that the property is insured to its replacement value (coinsurance provision).

Now, the coinsurance provision actually serves a useful purpose, as does the property/package policy itself. It is just so downright difficult to understand that you figure that it's useless to try and put the effort into it because the explanation is as confusing as the formula itself.

Not only will this confuse the dickens out of you, it will also send a chill down your spine because you'll get the funny feeling that you're underinsured but you won't know why. The good news is that, for the most part, you are probably not underinsured, although there may be some exclusion in there that you probably want to be made aware of.

What You Really Need to Know about Property

First off, know that's how insurance people refer to this policy—property.

"I'm not sure that would be covered under property."

"Let me switch you over to property; they would handle that…"

It is most valuable to note that this overview will enable you to determine the value of your property and make informed decisions about the proper coverage you need for your business. You must also know that the following discussion is the simplest explanation of property/package policies.

You should always refer back to this chapter as a reference when needed. This section is meant to be read over for its information, but it should be used primarily to refer to when you have a question and especially when you have a loss.

Your Owned Property Risk Analysis

Make a list of all the properties you own. Then make a list of all the properties you do not own yet you occupy and for which you must provide coverage.

First, let's look at the *owned property*. If you own a property, then the first thing you want to do is protect it from physical loss such as fire, wind, and so forth. These are the hazards that could sharply curtail your overall operations and cause great economic loss to the organization.

The most important aspect here, along with the elected coverage, is the determination of the value of the property. Some brokers will insure a property for the amount that it costs to purchase, adding between 2 and 5 percent each year for appreciation (appreciation on the cost of the materials and labor to repair or replace the damaged property). The insurer may ask you the price you paid for the property and whether you have a current appraisal on file.

"No? No appraisal? OK, then, we'll go with the purchase price."

This is wrong. Wrong! Wrong! Wrong!

The amount for which you purchased the property includes not only the building but also the land, which is generally perpetual.

Land does not depreciate and it generally cannot be destroyed. Therefore, if your house blows over, or is destroyed by fire or some other *covered* hazard, there needs to be enough insurance to replace the building.

If you insure the total value of the entire property, you will probably be overinsured. This will cost you additional premium, although I'd certainly rather be overinsured than underinsured.

Valuing Your Property

OK, how do you value your property? The easy way is to go to the land records and determine how the property is valued. If the land is assessed at 25 percent of the value of the entire property, and you purchased the property for $1 million, you can reasonably expect that the replacement cost of the building would be $750,000. Not only is this the easy way, it is also the wrong way.

The only proper way to value your property is to hire a certified commercial property appraiser to come in and appraise your property every two to five years. A commercial property appraiser will give you the market value of the property, the replacement value of the property, and the use value.

- The *market value* of the property is the amount for which you can reasonably expect to sell the property in the current commercial property market.

- The *replacement value* is the amount it costs to replace any insured structure should it sustain a catastrophic total loss.

- The *use value* is the amount of income you would lose if your property became uninhabitable or unusable for a period. If you both own and occupy the building, use value is valuable for internal purposes, but use value really should be insured if you are leasing the property. If the property becomes unusable and the occupants cannot use the property, your company will lose the income that is generated from the rental of that space.

That Coinsurance Thing

OK, now you have the replacement value of the property. Now, what the heck is this coinsurance thing?

The insurance industry recognizes that it is difficult to properly value a building's replacement value, but it also knows that it needs to add an incentive to ensure that the owner makes at least a good faith attempt to adequately insure the property. Thus, the insurer puts the coinsurance clause into this policy.

It is statistically very rare that a building is declared a total loss. A building usually is only partially destroyed, and therefore the entire limits of the policy are generally unnecessary if the building is properly insured.

The insurance company will pay up to the limits of the policy if the property is valued up to the coinsurance limit for the replacement value, which is generally 80 percent. Let's say, for example, you own a building with a replacement value of $1 million and a coinsurance amount of 80 percent. This means that as long as you have at least $800,000 in coverage on that building (again, the replacement value), the policy will pay 100 percent of the limits, or $800,000. The policy will not pay the entire loss if it is deemed a total loss, but because buildings are rarely total losses, the payment generally will be enough for the entire amount of the loss. It *will* pay 100 percent of all losses up to the $800,000 limit, and this should be enough insurance to cover most losses.

So, in this instance, if you have a $100,000 loss, the policy will pay the entire $100,000 loss after the deductible. If the deductible is $1,000, the payment for the loss would be $99,000.

Now let's say the building was only insured for $600,000, and the replacement value is $1 million. The insurance company would only pay the percentage difference between the actual coverage and the amount for which it should have been insured. So, if the replacement value is $1 million, the insured must have at least $800,000.

The percentage difference between the amount that is actually insured and the amount required to be insured is 75 percent ($600,000/$800,000).

Imagine that the insured loss is once again $100,000. Instead of paying $99,000, the insurance company will now pay only 75 percent of the loss ($75,000) minus the $1,000 deductible, or $74,000.

Therefore, it is quite valuable and, in my opinion, necessary to have timely appraisals done, especially in locations where the property is appreciating rapidly and creating a disparity between the value of the property and the replacement value. Although an appraisal can cost between $2,000 and $5,000 (and even more if you like the pretty pictures), it is worth it once you have a loss, because after a loss is the wrong time to figure out that your insurance is not sufficient to cover the loss. Come to think about it, insurance never seems to be worth it until you have a loss.

Let the Insurance Company Value the Property

If you're too cheap to hire your own appraiser, you can always ask your insurance company to send one. If the insurance company values the property, it may be bound by the value should you need the limits of the policy to pay a loss. Your insurance company can be held responsible for the entire amount of any claim if it sets the number.

The best bet is to insure the property at what you believe to be a good faith amount, hire the appraiser, and adjust as necessary.

I have found many a property that has been appraised for the total value of the property, including the land, which cannot be destroyed. Insuring only that which might need replacing helps reduce costs and save money. If you have a loss, the savings are much greater. If you don't have a loss, the savings are smaller, but the overall savings will be substantial nonetheless, and you will have the peace of mind that your property is adequately covered from the catastrophic loss.

You can also compel the insurer to appraise the property as a contingency to the insurance contract. I always try to get someone else to pay for things so my company doesn't have to pay. You'd be amazed at what some companies will help you out with if you ask.

If an insurance company refuses to appraise a property for its value and attempts to enforce the 80 percent coinsurance clause on the number of their choosing, you would have a case to get all the limits of the coverage should the limits set by the insurance carrier render the property underinsured. But the claim becomes just that—a case, which will need to be managed, negotiated, and possibly (probably) litigated. It's simply better to get the value figured out ahead of time.

Pay the money, hire the appraiser, and buy yourself and your company a little peace of mind. Remember, an appraisal will be necessary should you need to borrow against the property or if you want to find out the value prior to the sale of the property, so there are multiple justifications for getting one ahead of time. Not the least of which—you'll sleep better at night. You'll know the value and you can insure the replacement cost at a value that makes everyone happy.

Remember, these values are calculated on an occurrence basis, which means that losses that occur during the policy coverage period will be covered (assuming all other requirements are met). A great example of this distinction is illustrated in the World Trade Center bombings on 9/11. The group that bought the World Trade Center property (less than six months prior to the attacks) made two claims for the property damage, claiming that the two plane crashes were separate occurrences, and therefore they were entitled to policy limits for both occurrences.

A jury had first determined that the coordinated attack constituted only one occurrence. The issue, of course, is whether the second tower would have come down if the second plane had not hit it. If not, a strong case could be made that the attack comprised two separate occurrences, and the insured can collect the policy limits for both hits. If the attack were determined to have been one event, then the second plane, from an insurance standpoint, was incidental to the first loss, and therefore the entire loss would only be covered as a single occurrence.

The insurance company's basic argument was that the second tower would have come down even if the second plane hadn't hit it.

In December 2004, a federal jury sided with the ownership group and deemed this was in fact two occurrences and therefore the insurer would pay the policy limits for both occurrences.

Real Property versus Personal Property

This is a good time to explain the difference between real property and personal property.

Real property is any property that is permanently attached to the land or is permanently attached to the structure that is permanently attached to the ground. Real property also includes the land. Everything else is personal property.

So, for example, the ceiling fan you install becomes real property when it is attached to the ceiling, while the copy machine is considered personal property. You should have coverage for personal property as well as real property.

The first step in the process is to value all the personal property contained in and on the property. Equipment, furniture, computer hardware, and so forth should all be identified and quantified. If your company has furniture that is government surplus, the value might not be worth insuring at all. If the furniture or equipment is leased, it may be necessary to provide coverage under the terms of the lease. The rule of thumb is if you can't afford to lose it, insure it!

You can mitigate insurance costs by accepting a per-occurrence deductible and insuring any amount over that, up to the limits set forth in the policy. Setting up a maximum amount over the policy period (stop loss) will allow you to weather many smaller losses before coverage kicks in. The stop loss is the amount at which your insurance company begins to pay out in any one policy period, regardless of the number of claims in that same period.

There is also coverage for land-based risks related to transportation or communication (inland marine insurance). Inland marine covers property in transit or at other locations. Policies that cover mobile equipment are known as floaters. Mobile equipment used away from the company's premises requires a special (equipment) floater.

If the value of the equipment exceeds the maximum paid out on the policy, it may be valuable to insure the equipment for its actual cash value (schedule), which will ensure that the equipment is fully covered. This is similar to an auto policy but applies to equipment not classified as a motor vehicle.

On such a policy, you would actually name the piece of equipment (by providing a description to distinguish it as scheduled personal property) and record the replacement cost of the property. Because most blanket personal property coverage (miscellaneous coverage) has a maximum aggregate as well as a maximum per piece of equipment or property, the miscellaneous portion of the policy may cover only a portion of the high dollar machines or equipment.

If your location houses a mainframe computer, it would be wise to insure the computer equipment separately, and your company should elect coverage that protects against loss of information due to a hardware or power failure (electronic data processing (EDP) floater).

It is wise to back up your electronic data and transport that backup to an off-site location. If your organization has a network and depends on it for all aspects of its business, including communication, billing, and Web site advertising, it may be valuable to consider setting up a second mainframe that can help to speed up the flow of business in the short term and can also serve as a backup should the central mainframe go down.

This is a risk-control technique known as duplication.

Your organization may also suffer losses if a location is damaged for an extended period. For this reason, it is essential to ensure that this loss will not affect the overall future operations of the organization. The package policy provides for coverage to compensate the insured for the loss of business in addition to the cost of repair (business income coverage—BIC).

Your company can also elect coverage in case a supplier sustains a loss and is unable to deliver a product or service essential for the production of your product or service (contingent business income exposures). If the breakdown of your organization's equipment could potentially harm the continuity of its operations, there is coverage to help offset losses that can occur from this type of loss (equipment breakdown insurance).

For example, imagine you are in the business of mass producing superhero action figures. You have a machine that connects the Insurance Guy (he's my favorite) head to both his torso and the Insurance Guy cape (because, let's face it, the Insurance Guy is not really the Insurance Guy without his cape).

If this machine breaks down, and the entire Insurance Guy doll-making line goes down, equipment breakdown coverage will help to offset loss of income due to the breakdown of the machine.

Now, let's say that you get your Insurance Guy head and cape combination from a manufacturer in Taiwan. A typhoon wipes out the factory, and—wham, no more Insurance Guy heads. Losses would occur because of this type of interruption and would be covered under the contingent business income coverage. And you can't use the head and cape of the more popular Insurance Girl action figure on the Insurance Guy's body. That would be wrong.

Remember, most package policies cover every type of loss except for those occurrences that are specifically excluded (all risks policy). Review the policy, make sure all owned property is covered, and then look over the exclusions in the policy to determine whether there is anything there that needs to be covered. If you find something in the exclusions, especially something you *thought* was covered, check the endorsements to see whether it was added in. If not, call your broker and add it on.

This overview cannot begin to address your organization's needs in this area, but if you understand what your needs are and what is available in the marketplace, you will be better able to determine whether you are properly covered.

These are merely examples of standard package policy coverage you can elect. This is not a comprehensive list because you can insure any exposure that may be subject to a loss. Remember, most companies don't know whether they are properly covered until *after* they sustain a loss. By then, it's usually too late.

11
Insurance 101 — General Liability

A Road Map

Do you suffer from insomnia? Do the pressures of your day keep you awake at night? Are you tired of taking prescription sleep medication? Have I got a cure for you—a surefire solution that is tried and true. In fact, I have tried it myself, and it works great.

Make a copy of your company's general liability policy, place it on your nightstand at home, and read it before bed. Don't skip any words, commas, sentences, or paragraphs. If you read a portion of the text but don't understand it, go back and reread it. You will be sound asleep before you get past the second page.

OK, insurance policies are not the most stimulating reading material in the world. After all, they are legal contracts, and legal contracts are written so that they can be understood and interpreted only by attorneys. That's how lawyers make their money. They prepare documents so confusing that only other lawyers have any chance of figuring out what they mean.

General Liability—What It Covers

Commercial general liability is generally referred to as "slip and fall" coverage. This comes from the retail industry, which has a high volume of customer traffic on its premises, and general liability will cover losses that occur from injuries occurring to customers and any other nonemployee.

Commercial general liability (GL or CGL) is needed to cover you and your company from any actions that occur when someone unrelated to the company comes onto your property or property in your control and is injured. It also covers losses if someone cuts through the parking lot and trips and falls and claims the injury is due to your negligence ("If that parking lot weren't there, I wouldn't have had to cut through it and I wouldn't have fallen. Give me $200,000, and we'll call it even").

General liability will also cover an organization from actions that allegedly arise due to the negligence of you or your employee working off-site. For example, if you have a crew doing repairs at an occupied building, the building owner will generally require that your company name the building owner on your general liability policy (additional insured). Then the building owner would be protected from any claims that arise due to the negligent act of your employees.

Structure of the General Liability Policy

The first page (declaration page) of the policy describes the amount of coverage, as well as when the policy starts and ends (policy period) and the cost (premium).

There are generally two types of insurance (coverage forms) having to do with the treatment of claims reporting. The most common form is the coverage in which claims occurring within the policy period are covered, regardless of when the claim is reported (occurrence form). This is the most common form, and is probably the form you have in place right now.

An alternative policy form covers only those claims reported during the policy period or for an extended period established by the terms of the policy (claims made coverage form). Claims made policies are utilized to limit the amount of time into the future that a claim can be reported. This is important if your organization has an exposure for which a claim may not be reported for years after the claim has occurred.

Next is the amount of coverage (limits of insurance). Limits of insurance is the maximum the insurance company will pay. It is usually broken down as follows:

- The maximum amount paid for each occurrence (each occurrence limit).

- The total amount that can be paid during the policy period (general aggregate limit).

- The total amount that can be paid for intentional acts such as libel, slander, and false imprisonment (personal and advertising injury limit). Personal and advertising injury limits are separate from the limits of the GL.

- Total amount that will be paid for the physical damage to property rented by your company (damages to premises rented to you limit).

- More limited coverage for fire damage (fire legal liability limit).

- Coverage for exposures arising from faulty work or product manufacture (products-completed operations aggregate limit). This means if you build, repair, or manufacture something, and someone is injured as a result of specifications not being met, it would be covered here.

The next section on the declarations is the cost of the policy (premium), which breaks down as follows:

- The full amount of the policy at the beginning of the policy (total advance premium), which is based on an estimate of either payroll or gross receipt multiplied by the rate (annual minimum premium). This is calculated using the payroll of those who are directly responsible for the work (direct employees) *and* their supervisors, or is based on total gross revenues, which may or may not be an accurate barometer of your company's loss exposure in the marketplace.

Please note that I highlighted direct employees and their direct supervisors. The reason for this is due to the assumption that supervisors of direct employees are in the field as well as the line workers, and the possibility of their actions leading to a claim for negligence is just as high as that of direct employees.

Auditable Policy

Most general liability policies are auditable policies, meaning that an estimate of the exposure basis, such as direct labor payroll or gross revenues (premium basis) is made at the beginning of the policy and then the actual numbers are calculated after the policy period ends. For example, if your GL policy is based on payroll and you estimate your payrolls to be $1 million, and on audit it is found that the payroll was $1.2 million (or $200,000 higher), you will pay additional premium on the extra payroll.

Most GL policies have a minimum premium, which means if you underestimate your payroll, you will be assessed the additional premium upon audit. If you overestimate your premium at inception, you still pay the annual minimum. *You do not receive a refund!*

Most general liability policies have a minimum premium amount, which is based on an estimate of the premium basis at the beginning of the policy.

Do not let your insurer estimate the premium basis.

Use conservative numbers, and if the insurer or broker questions the numbers or tries to apply their own set of numbers, do not allow them to do it unless they also agree to waive the minimum premium requirement. The estimate of premium is just that: an estimate. You should endeavor to come in lower than the minimum to avoid a penalty for overestimating.

Most policies have a minimum premium equal to the initial estimated (advance) premium, so be careful here also. It is an incentive to accurately estimate your payroll less between 5 and 10 percent to account for fluctuations in your payroll status. If it is apparent that your payroll is going to be higher, you will pay the additional premium on audit.

I cannot emphasize this enough: if your estimate is higher than the audited premium, and the advance premium is the minimum, you will *not* receive a credit (refund).

This is extremely important. Many organizations will attempt to estimate their premium basis as closely as possible to avoid a hefty additional payment in the next year. Many companies do not even realize that they are paying a minimum premium and anticipate a refund when the premium basis falls below the advance premium. It is usually when this scenario plays out that they realize they don't get that refund.

The bottom line: do not overestimate your payrolls or revenues. Do not be overly optimistic for the next policy period. Circumstances beyond your control could cause these numbers to be lower than anticipated. Naturally, if this occurs, the company will probably be in a position where they could use the additional cash that was paid on the minimum premium.

There is also a minimum you pay for the coverage if you cancel early (minimum earned premium at inception). This means if you get the policy today and cancel it in a week, you will pay this amount, which is generally between 30 and 40 percent of the total advance premium. You pay this premium regardless of the amount of time the insurance is in place—even if you cancel within days. The reasoning for both of these provisions is sound from a business standpoint. The insurance company needs the financial protection to avoid having the policy cancelled early and replaced with another policy shortly after the beginning (effective date) of the policy.

If these provisions were not in the policy, the insured could use the executed policy to negotiate a better deal even after the company has entered into an agreement to put the coverage in place (binder). For example, if a company binds a policy with Carrier A and receives a significantly better quote from Carrier B after the policy period starts, a minimum earned premium at inception makes it detrimental to the insured to immediately cancel Carrier A's policy and replace it with Carrier B's policy. The insured would owe premium equivalent for the first three or four months of the policy, which in almost all cases would negate the discounted premium from Carrier B.

Once the policy is in force past a contractually agreed upon minimum, the advance premium would be forfeited by the insured.

Although this is to protect the insurance carrier, it's just good business. Your company should be aware that these provisions exist and how they could affect the company. Just as you, the insured, need protection from the insurance carrier, the insurer needs to be protected from the potentially damaging actions of you, the insured.

The next page (forms schedule) is generally the page that shows the documents that change or amends the basic language of the standard or boilerplate policy (endorsements).

Covered, Excluded = Product

General liability policies are characterized more by what they don't cover than by what they do. It is valuable to explain how this evolved. Commercial general liability coverage will generally cover those events that are not specifically excluded in the policy. As the work environment evolves, unanticipated loss exposures will occur, which will be initially covered by the policy. Because they are unanticipated, these loss exposures are obviously not excluded.

A good example of this is sexual harassment and hostile work environment exposures. Although more and more women began to enter the workforce in the early 1970s, the insurance industry did not anticipate that sexual harassment exposure would evolve. When these claims began to occur, they were covered under general liability only because they were not excluded under the policy. The insurance industry soon began to exclude this coverage to avoid paying for losses they had not intended to pay.

Once sexual harassment became an exclusion, there was actually a period during which this coverage could not be easily purchased. The property casualty industry smartened up pretty quickly, though, and began to offer coverage for harassment claims as a separate policy (stand-alone policy).

And that, ladies and gentlemen, is the way it works in insurance.

A new unanticipated loss exposure is covered under CGL. Once identified, the loss exposure becomes an exclusion on future policies. Then it's turned into a product. Sexual harassment has been packaged with other workplace loss exposures and has evolved into a very necessary cover for businesses as well as a highly profitable product for the insurance industry (employment practices liability insurance [EPLI]). Insurance companies have found that policies with the word *sex* in their titles generally do not sell too well overall, which is one reason they sell them under *EPLI,* a name without any sexual connotation.

When you read your general liability policy, look over the list of events that are not covered (exclusions). If there is a loss exposure that needs to be covered, check the endorsements to see whether the coverage has been added. If an endorsement is not attached, do not fret. The insurance company will be more than happy to provide it to you—for a fee, of course.

If your organization has this type of policy, the easiest way to determine your coverage is to look at the exclusions and see what is not covered. Then look at the endorsements (generally in the back of the insurance policy) to see whether an exposure is covered by endorsement. Endorsements can also be added to exclude coverage specifically included in the basic policy.

If you determine that a loss exposure you need to be covered is not covered, call the insurer or your broker. If the insurer is unable to add it to the policy, he will be more than happy to sell you an additional policy that does provide this insurance. The amount you pay to cover a potential loss will never be worth it so long as you don't have a loss. But when you do have a loss, there is pretty much no price you wouldn't have paid to insure against it.

Commercial General Liability—Got to Have It

Commercial general liability is essential to the continued operations of the company. Like all other types of coverage with limited loss activity, the organization will generally not see the need for this coverage until a claim actually occurs. Often, this is the first clue your company has in finding out that its coverage will not cover a loss it thought it did, and that makes for a very uncomfortable few days. This can also make the difference between a business thriving or just struggling to survive.

Most companies require general liability before they do business with other companies, especially if the product or service is on their customer's premises. This protects the clients, who don't have any intimate knowledge of the other company's work environment, procedures, and training. Insurance gives them this protection. The only other alternative is to conduct business in a vacuum, and that is a difficult environment in which to generate a profit.

Find out what amount of coverage your clients require and try to purchase at least that amount. It will serve you well to have sufficient and continuous coverage in place, instead of trying to argue with the client about the amount of coverage you have versus the amount of coverage you need.

In Business, It's Good to Make a Favorable First Impression

12
Insurance 101 — Workers' Compensation

It's Mandatory, Even When It Isn't

All businesses with employees should carry workers' compensation (work comp) coverage. In fact, work comp is mandatory in all states. Some states, however, allow exemptions for organizations that have less than a given minimum number of employees. Regardless, any such exemption does not negate your organization's responsibility to provide medical care and indemnification to an employee injured while on the job.

The same rationale applies to workers' compensation as applies to personal health coverage: you just never know when someone will get injured, what the extent of the injury will be, and how severe the effect will be on your continued operations.

If you think that you can handle a loss because you only have few employees or the only employee is your brother-in-law, think again. An employee who suffers a debilitating loss while on the job could devastate your company economically if you don't have coverage. Depending on the structure of your organization, such a loss could financially affect you both professionally and personally.

Employee injuries can be as small as a cut finger, which may require on-site first aid, or a devastating injury or illness, which could totally disable the employee for an extended period. In some cases, an injury can be so severe that it renders that employee permanently disabled. These more serious cases tend to remain open for years and years ("long tail" or lingering claim). In fact, if an employee is considered to be permanently disabled, you could be on the hook for the length of the employee's life.

You also need workers' compensation coverage if your company enters into agreements and needs to provide insurance coverage to meet contractual obligations. Most companies will not do business with other companies unless the proper coverage is in place, and work comp coverage is a necessity in all but the smallest jobs. Even if you are a sole proprietor, and even if you are exempt by state law because of your company's size, you will severely limit your customer base if you do not have workers' compensation.

The biggest problem most companies have with workers' compensation is that it can be rife with fraud, especially in the lower-paying end of the employment spectrum. There are many employees who would rather get paid two-thirds of their wages to stay home and watch reruns on TV than toil on an assembly line or work manual labor out in the hot sun.

Although many employees are legitimately injured the first time a job-related injury claim is filed, some decide that they like this coverage so much that they make a career out of it, going from job to job, getting "injured," and going through the system again and again.

Hey, it beats working.

It is very frustrating to the employer when an injury or illness occurs. A claim affects all aspects of an organization in an adverse, almost poisonous way. A claim increases premium costs, depletes the workforce, and adds to the cost when an injured employee's position needs to be filled. The employer must also give the injured employee his or her job back when the employee is completely rehabilitated or can partially perform (light duty), and this can sometimes lead to additional staffing costs.

Fraud in Workers' Compensation Claims

There are many reasons for fraud related to workplace injuries:

- Workers' compensation is designed to protect the employee from the employer. That is why it's required. Just as there are some employees who perpetuate fraud, there are some employers who take advantage of their position of power over an employee to coerce that employee into not making a claim for a legitimate workplace injury. This is as it should be. The employee should be able to claim for a work-related injury, although the idea of giving the benefit of the doubt to the employee in almost every instance can be quite frustrating to the employer.

- Workers' compensation boards and commissions are heavily employee biased, which means the burden of proof is upon the employer

- Claims may be difficult to prove because most claims are soft tissue injuries, such as lower back and neck strains, and are difficult to validate and substantiate. It makes it difficult for the employer to prove an employee is really not hurt if there are no tests to prove the nature and extent of the injury, even when the employee claims the pain is so severe that he or she is unable to perform work-related duties.

Yet, there are many simple and effective strategies to create a great deal of savings in this area.

As you probably already know, there is a whole industry of attorneys, doctors, and other health care practitioners who make their livings treating work-related (occupational) injuries. As I mentioned earlier, a claimant/plaintiff/employee can never accurately evaluate the extent of his injury until he talks to his lawyer. The longer the patient treats, the longer that employee is out of work, and this enhances the value of the claim, which in turn enhances an attorney's portion of any settlement.

I once received a call from an attorney representing an employee who allegedly was injured on the job. The employee had called this attorney, claiming he was injured on the job, a claim that could not be substantiated by witnesses or any physical evidence. He had called the attorney on his cell phone *from the ambulance!*

The attorney had placards all over the airport soliciting work-related cases. It seems this guy had staged the injury after writing the lawyer's name and number down, and off we go.

A workers' compensation policy is coverage that protects the employer from financial loss due to a work-related injury to an employee. This coverage is afforded to employees regardless of fault. Most policies will provide the statutory minimum amount, although the policy may have an amount in excess of this. This provision will cover up to the maximum limit if compelled and spells out in full the terms under which the maximum would be paid (employer's liability) if the work comp piece of the policy does not pay or the minimum statutory limits are exhausted.

Please note that the states control and regulate insurance, each with its own different laws and requirements. You will need to confirm the requirements of the states or jurisdictions in which you do business to see whether you are complying with state-mandated minimum work comp insurance requirements.

Classification of Employees

Employees are classified by the type of work they do (classification of operations) and are assigned a "code number." Employees who participate directly in the manufacture of a product or delivery of a service (direct employees) are at the highest risk to suffer injury, and therefore the employer pays the highest rate in work comp for these employees. As the risk increases, so does the rate.

Employees whose primary work function is in an office (code 8810) are at the lowest risk and therefore are the least expensive to insure. Salespeople, drivers, and supervisors fall into varying classifications between these codes.

The Scopes Manual

Each classification is assigned based on the description of work duties that fit with the description assigned by NCCI through the Scopes Manual. It is valuable to evaluate each employee to determine whether each employee is properly classified.

For example, a foreman or supervisor is included in the same labor class as direct employees. However, if this supervisor does not have direct supervisory authority over these employees, but manages and supervises a number of job sites or locations, he would be classified as an executive supervisor, and the rate for that classification is between 65 and 80 percent less than the direct class.

If you assume that this supervisor makes $50,000 per year, then moving only this supervisor from a direct class to a supervisory class could save you anywhere between $6,000 and $10,000 in premium (depending on the state and the type of work being done)—for one employee!

Premium Calculation

At the commencement of the policy, the employer is asked to estimate the amount of payroll for each class of employee. The amount of payroll in each class (premium basis) is then multiplied by the rate and divided by each $100 of payroll to get the initial premium (unmodified premium). There are various other fees added to this total, such as the fee to increase the premium from the statutory minimum (increase limits), a discount based on the size of the payroll (premium discount), terrorism, and any additional coverage either elected by the employer or mandated by law.

The Experience Modification (EMR), or "Mod Rate"

In the middle of all this (after the unmodified premium but before the additional credits and debits mentioned above) is the all-important mod rate (experience modification rate [EMR]). This rate is calculated in most states by the National Council on Compensation Insurance (NCCI). There are a few states that calculate their own rate (monopolistic states and non-NCCI states; monopolistic states are Washington, North Dakota, Ohio, West Virginia, and Wyoming).

The EMR weighs industry norms for number (frequency) and amount (severity) of claims to develop a factor based on total payrolls. If it is calculated that your experience is worse than the industry average (average is 1.00), your company is assigned a mod rate in excess of 1.00, and the amount over 1.00 becomes a percentage surcharge. If, on the other hand, your history is deemed by the formula to be better than the average, the mod rate will be less than 1.00, and that percentage difference is returned as a credit.

To illustrate this, let's say your unmodified premium comes to a total of $100,000. Your organization has been assigned a mod rate of 1.10. The mod rate applies a 10 percent surcharge, or an additional premium amount in this case of $10,000 for a total premium of $110,000. If your mod rate instead is 0.90, you would receive a 10 percent discount, and the $100,000 premium would be discounted to $90,000.

As you can see, the mod rate can have a great effect on your insurance costs. Your costs directly correlate to the claims reported to the insurance company, who in turn report them to NCCI. NCCI values the frequency of claims more heavily than the severity, as each claim is capped at a predetermined amount.

Workers' Compensation Strategies

Many companies will report all claims to the insurance company, regardless of the severity of the injury. Although this is a viable strategy, it will adversely affect your mod rate.

Use the following points to adopt a better strategy:

- If an employee claims an injury on the job, always have the person taken for emergency care immediately.

- Have the employee taken to the hospital by another employee. Do not have the employee seek emergency care on his or her own, and do not wait to provide medical attention.

- Do not worry about the paperwork. The injury and medical treatment for that injury are the priority. Many years back, I had a manager call to let me know that one of his employees had cut his hand and he was bleeding profusely. When I inquired whether he was at the hospital, the manager said he was going to take him, but he couldn't find the forms he needed to fill out for the claim.

- After treatment, take the injured employee home, and pay the employee for a full day.

- Pay for the initial treatment up front. If the claim ends there, it's one less claim going to the insurance company. If not, it will mitigate the amount of the claim, or you can always turn it in to the insurance carrier later. The carrier may give you some grief about late reporting, but they still have to cover the claim.

- If you don't want to pay for the initial service, have the provider send the bills to you. If they insist on workers' compensation information, have the provider send the bills to you so you can forward them to the insurance company. This will again give you the option of turning the claim in to the carrier after you determine the severity of the loss.

- Most states have a waiting period of between 3 and 7 days before lost wage compensation kicks in. In most states, the employer does not have to pay the employee during this waiting period. My advice, however, is to pay the employee! There is no better way of alienating an employee than denying him the pay that he loses due to a work-related injury.

- Get a list of preferred doctors for your geographical area from the work comp carrier. When you turn this in to the insurance company, they will have less of a problem with the ongoing course of treatment if you send the injured employee to their doctors.

- Document everything. When in doubt, turn it in to the carrier immediately.

Miscellaneous Provisions within the Work Comp Policy

Some other important amendments to the workers' compensation policy (endorsements) are modifications/requirements of the states in which your organization operates. There is also an important endorsement for work done in states other than the ones in which you are located (other states or limited other states endorsement). This will cover employees who travel to other states to conduct business on a casual basis.

For example, here in Virginia, companies do business in the District of Columbia and Maryland, but because they return each night to Virginia, they are covered under Virginia statutes.

It is important to note that if an employee is injured in another jurisdiction, he or she has the option of claiming for benefits in either state. Therefore, if a Virginia-based employee travels to Maryland and is injured, the employee can choose one of the two states in which to file benefits. This decision is generally based on which state has the more generous benefits, and, of course, where the employee's lawyer is licensed to do business.

The limited other states endorsement will cover the employee if the travel is incidental and not ongoing. Thus, if the office is in one state, and workers travel to another state from time to time to conduct business-related activities, work comp losses that occur in this other state will be covered. However, if the employee goes to another state and sets up shop there for a few weeks or months, it may be best to get coverage in that state to avoid coverage issues when a claim occurs. The insurer may try to deny the claim based on the less-than-temporary nature of the work.

As you can see, this is an area in which you can achieve a high degree of savings. By putting these strategies together with knowledge of your coverage, you will be able to effectively manage your workers' compensation claims and enjoy the savings that comes with the knowledge and understanding of the policy, the system, and the way in which to effectively work within the system.

Please understand that each state may have different reporting requirements and other requirements unique to that jurisdiction. It is imperative that you learn the nuances of each state in which you have work activities. When in doubt, turn the claim into your carrier immediately to ensure that the employee is afforded the best care available, which will help to minimize the rehabilitation period, and will get the employee healthy and back to work as soon as possible.

So, get yourself a Scopes Manual, look through it, and…

Let the Savings Begin!

13

Insurance 101 — Miscellaneous Insurance Coverage

Umbrella, EPLI, D&O, E&O, and Environmental

Now that you have been exposed to the basics of insurance coverage that are used by all companies in the marketplace, it will be valuable to look at certain other optional coverage that may or may not fit the needs of your company. Keep in mind that any need and any loss exposure you have can be insured for a price. That having been said, this chapter will not be a comprehensive study of all additional coverage.

Instead, I will endeavor to give you an overview of the common additional insurance coverage out in the insurance marketplace so you can make informed and cost-effective decisions. It is also valuable to note that many organizations decide against purchasing coverage for which they have an exposure. This is based on the theory that if they have the coverage, they are opening themselves up to claims for it. This may be true in some instances, and this reasoning can even be the determining factor when a business is on the fence over whether to purchase a particular coverage.

I do not particularly agree with this for the following reasons:

- *The reason you get insurance*—because the financial consequences of the loss are not tolerable (the loss cannot be financed without insurance) and the potential for loss, however remote it may be, still exists. If you know that you will be exposed to that risk sometime in the future, then you should know that you need to take steps to mitigate the financial consequences of that potential loss to ensure the future of your organization.

- *The reason you don't get insurance*—because you either believe it will never happen to you or that you can handle it if it does

- ***You'll never know until you know***—when a claim occurs, you will never know whether you are being exposed due to the existence of the applicable insurance. If the company is willing to take the risk, then it is probably in the position to self-insure the risk. If it is a risk that does not occur too often, and the company can take proactive steps to mitigate the chances of a loss, self-insurance may be preferable to purchasing additional coverage.

Employment practices liability coverage is a good example. Most companies would prefer not to get the coverage and instead enforce a stringent policy against such actions as sexual harassment, discriminatory employment practices, and allegations of wrongful discharge. These measures do not eliminate the risk, but such companies have taken risk-control steps to mitigate the possibility of this type of loss.

I have not been able to document a claim that was filed solely on the basis that there was coverage available to cover it, unless it involved fraud by a party to the insurance contract, which is a whole different story. It has been my experience that if someone sues you for $10 million and you have limits of only $5 million, most folks will take those limits and run.

This is sound reasoning when you are deciding on higher limits, but the actual purchase of insurance rarely creates an exposure by itself. Thus, the bottom line is to make your decisions based on the exposures you have and not because of the potential that the mere existence of coverage might get your company sued.

If you need to decide on higher limits, find out where the price point is that results in the greatest cost savings and then make your decisions accordingly. For example, you may need $5 million in limits, but there is a huge price difference between $4 million and $5 million. It may be that $5 million is the price point at which the price for higher limits diminishes, so you might be able to get between $8 and $10 million for a nominal additional premium.

One last note on this subject—if someone has a valid claim against you that has a value of $2 million or $20 million, you're in real deep either way. The expectations from the other side increase when there are higher limits, but most claims will settle within whatever limits you have, as long as the insurance you are carrying is perceived by a claimant and society as a whole as adequate.

Regardless of how you perceive and value your company, there aren't too many people who want to take the keys from you. Most, if not all, just want the cash.

It is also important to investigate each claim to find mitigating circumstances that may cause the other party's expectations to be lowered. The very existence of coverage does not itself create the hazard, and excess coverage will not help to mitigate that loss.

Imagine the havoc that would ensue if you had a multimillion dollar loss, but your company had decided not to cover the loss exposure because it would invite claims. It would be pretty foolish not to get coverage if the plaintiff reasonably expects to get more than—say—nothing!

Miscellaneous Insurance Coverage

When insuring high or unique loss exposures and risks, insurance may not be available through a carrier licensed to do business in your state (admitted carrier). States will allow insurance companies that are not licensed in that particular state (non-admitted carrier) to sell coverage through designated specialty licensed brokers (surplus lines).

Surplus lines brokers are allowed to sell policies issued by non-admitted carriers under the following conditions:

- The broker has a surplus lines license and resides in the state

- The coverage afforded by the non-admitted carrier is not available from admitted carriers

- The non-admitted carrier is deemed to be acceptable to the state

Surplus lines are generally used for risks that are beyond the scope of admitted carriers, such as umbrella liability, professional liability, and employment practices liability.

The easiest way to figure out whether your policy is a surplus lines policy (besides reading the policy, of course) is to note whether you paid surplus lines tax on the policy.

Admitted carriers pay into a fund that protects the insured from insolvency of any admitted carrier (state guaranty fund). The guaranty fund typically will pay after all other insurance is exhausted. The state guaranty fund does not protect the insured from the insolvency of a non-admitted carrier.

If your organization decides to use a non-admitted carrier, make sure it is rated for financial strength by the industry (A.M. Best rating) of A+ or better. This rating is usually followed by a Roman numeral from I to XV that indicates the carrier's financial size (Class XV is the largest). So a company rated A+ XV would have the high rating for financial strength and the largest capacity to handle large losses.

Should a company have a rating of A-or lower, it should be used only after careful consideration. Although A-carriers are still generally very strong, some companies will not do business with another company unless their insurance is on "A" rated paper or better.

A lower-rated company normally needs to price its products lower to offset the lower rating, which can compound its financial problems. And if it's a nonadmitted carrier, it's essential that it be a financially sound company, since there is no state protection from its insolvency.

Umbrella Liability

You can elect to have umbrella liability as a cost-effective way of extending your liability limits over multiple policies. Umbrella coverage is different than excess liability because excess liability adds additional limits over one existing policy. Umbrella policies have the additional features of providing insurance coverage for which there is no underlying coverage and will, in fact, take the primary position. Some umbrella policies will also replace coverage should the primary insurer become insolvent (drop down).

Most excess and umbrella companies do not intend to pay claims, so if drop down coverage is afforded, it is usually only when the primary policy has a super rated A+ carrier with a large capacity, to negate the possibility of having to drop down in the place of an insolvent primary carrier.

Umbrella coverage can be placed over most primary policies and is a cost-effective way of meeting contractual liability requirements. For example, let's say your company has a GL policy with a one-time maximum limit (per occurrence) of $1 million and a total amount that can be paid out per the policy period (general aggregate) of $2 million. Then you have an umbrella with a limit of $5 million under the primary policy. The umbrella limits extend the primary limits and provide a total of $6 million per occurrence and $7 million general aggregate.

This gives your organization a cost-effective way of providing evidence of sufficient insurance prior to the execution of any contracts, which gives the company a leg up when competing for business. Oh yeah, it also provides for larger loss exposures.

Most businesses these days won't consider doing work with companies who cannot provide proof of insurance up front. This coverage is invaluable and can be used by your sales force as an effective marketing tool, because it exhibits stability.

Professional/Errors and Omissions (E&O) Liability

Professional liability insurance protects the professional from legal liability arising from claims that allege an individual failed to use the care, skill, and education expected from a professional, such as an engineer, architect, or insurance professional. If you are required to keep this insurance in place, look carefully to see whether there is a clause in which the insured agrees to adhere to an out-of-court settlement (consent to settle provision).

In professional liability cases, as in all liability cases, it may be appropriate and cost effective to settle a claim even when it has little merit (nuisance claim). In professional liability cases, though, a willingness to settle could be perceived as an admission of culpability on the professional's part, which could cause irreparable harm to his or her reputation. If settling a case will put you out of business, regardless of fault, you may not be inclined to settle even the smallest of cases. Most carriers will agree to delete the consent to settle provision by endorsement for a fee.

Errors and omissions (E&O) liability limits coverage to liability arising from negligent acts, errors, and omissions, and will not cover intentional acts.

Employment Practices Liability (EPLI)

EPLI is a great example of a policy that was not anticipated by the industry. General liability generally covers everything (all risks) and then excludes all the stuff it doesn't want to cover (exclusion) or adds in coverage (endorsement). What cannot be added will be sold under a separate, stand-alone policy for an additional price.

Claims for sexual harassment began as more and more women entered the work force in the 1970s. The changing political climate also asserted the rights of minorities in the workplace and made it increasingly difficult for employers to wrongfully harass, discriminate against, or discharge an employee for any reason other than cause.

When the general liability market was hit by these additional unforeseen claims arising from this changing cultural climate, they covered and defended them under the CGL policy because these loss exposures had never been specifically excluded. In reaction, the industry began to exclude these claims from its general liability policies. For a time, it was almost impossible to get coverage for these exposures.

The insurance industry caught on quickly, though, and began offering coverage. This evolved into Employment Practices Liability Insurance (EPLI), which encompassed a host of loss exposures that could occur due to the employee-employer relationship and the conflicts that could arise from the motivation or perceived motivation of the employer in the hiring or involuntary termination of an employee.

The major issue in EPLI is the qualifications for coverage. Most insurers will only cover organizations that divulge any prior claims within a certain time frame, usually the past five to ten years. Failure to provide this information could preclude coverage.

Most companies who try to qualify for EPLI coverage have never had coverage in this area due to cost or the unavailability of coverage, and they were forced to settle these claims internally and outside of insurance. Most of these cases are settled expeditiously and confidentially, and these companies are reluctant to air out this type of information for fear it may become public and generate more claim activity. Many companies would rather not pay for insurance that won't cover a future loss if they have to dredge up past indiscretions and risk the negative publicity associated with this information out in the open, should this qualifying information ever get out.

EPLI is a valuable policy to have because the cost of defending a case can be very expensive and the tendency of the legal system again is to give the benefit of the doubt to the alleged aggrieved employee. Then again, as stated earlier in this chapter, a comprehensive and ongoing campaign within the organization to manage employee behaviors in the workplace will help to mitigate these types of losses.

Many managers have told me over the years things like "That's the way we talk around here—people understand that," and, "She knows I don't mean nothin' by that!"

These folks are looking for trouble.

On the other hand, it is essential to train managers on the proper procedures for documenting substandard work performance that may lead to termination of employment, so the employee will have little ammunition should he or she decide to assert an EPLI claim to save his or her job or enhance the separation package from the organization.

Directors and Officers (D&O) Coverage

A directors and officers coverage policy protects the named directors and officers of an organization from any claims arising from a negligent act, error, omission, breach of duty, misstatement, or misleading statement (wrongful acts).

This insurance generally has two parts.

- The first reimburses the company for any losses due to wrongful acts (corporate reimbursement coverage).

- The second covers the director or officer for any claims he or she is legally obligated to pay due to a wrongful act, and the company is not obligated to pay on behalf of the director or officer (direct coverage).

D&O coverage is generally used in publicly held companies, although it may have uses in a privately held organization. It is commonly believed that D&O, more than any other coverage, opens up a privately owned company to more claims.

Crime Policy

Crime policies are pretty straightforward, covering losses from the following actions:

- Employee dishonesty
- Forgery or alteration
- Theft, disappearance, and destruction
- Robbery and safe burglary
- Computer fraud and wire transfer
- Money order and counterfeit currency
- Credit card forgery

One of the more valuable endorsements to a crime policy is one that provides security for plans that require a bond (fidelity bond) for compliance with ERISA (Employee Retirement Income Security Act) to indemnify programs such as pension and welfare plans. Although this type of coverage provides much-needed protection, its value as mandated security for benefits programs alone makes the policy worthwhile. It also adds protection from the unlawful acts of employees out of the office, such as on service calls to the home or the premises of another.

If your employee steals something, the organization would be covered for the actions of its employee.

Environmental Liability

This coverage provides for first and third party claims to manage pollution-related loss exposures. This can sometimes be contained in a commercial general liability and pollution (environmental impairment liability [EIL]) policy to avoid gaps in coverage. First party coverage is for losses to the insured property, while third party coverage protects the insured against pollution claims for property damage and bodily injury to others.

In other words, if your organization releases contaminants into the environment that lead to a loss, environmental liability will cover this type of loss.

The following are some specific coverages that are available in environmental policies:

- UST (underground storage tank) compliance

- Remediation stop loss

- Environmental remediation

- Asbestos abatement

- Site-specific and contractors EIL

- Environmental E&O liability

Environmental liability should be tailored to your company's specific needs and should be elected only when there is a real threat of environmental contaminant release that would be attributable to the organization. This coverage is required if you manufacture or transport hazardous materials and their byproducts, but it should also be used when you have a gas tank underground and the potential for a leak and the subsequent cleanup needs to be funded.

Disclaimer

Remember, all loss exposures are insurable, with few exceptions. If you follow the risk-management model, you should be able to easily determine what your needs are and whether the coverage is necessary.

Only *you* know your business, and you know it better than anyone else. When you break it down to its most basic terms, you will find that you possess the knowledge to determine your own insurance needs, and you won't need to rely on any outside sources to determine whether *your* needs are protected.

Also, this is not a comprehensive list of available coverage out in the insurance marketplace. On the contrary, there are many other insurance policies that you can elect to take that are not covered here.

It's Your Money. Keep More of It!

14
How to Talk Insurance Like You Know What You're Talking About

How to Sound Like an Insurance Pro

There are some topics that come up from time to time which are thrust onto the front pages. If you're like I was when I first started out, these issues seem rather mundane. In fact, to the untrained eye, they don't appear to be all that newsworthy.

If you really want to convince people, especially insurance folks, that you know the market and you know insurance, there are certain issues that will come up in conversation, and everyone seems to know what they're talking about, but again, it seems rather—well—Greek to you. Instead of sitting there nodding and trying not to nod off, brush up on the following topics, which come up from time to time. If they don't, bring them up yourself. Insurance people will sit and take notice even if they don't agree with what you are saying. You need to understand, though, that the views I take are those of a business insurance consumer, and these views are mine and mine alone.

If the discussion becomes heated, just settle them down, remind them that you're the customer, and they should at least pretend to agree with you at some point.

The Myth of the Hard Market

The hard market is the stuff of legend as far as I'm concerned. To me, it appears to be a cyclical and arbitrary theory promulgated by the insurance company to justify the need for increased premiums to fuel shortfalls caused by free market conditions and certain disasters that adversely affect the insurance industry.

But that's just me.

First, let me say that there may have been a time that the theory of a hard or soft market may have been justified. I've only been in the business since 1986, but the research on the issue is a little sketchy.

From what I have gathered, soft markets, in which insurance premiums drop and the market is more advantageous to the buyer, generally lasted two to five years and would follow the cyclical trends of the economy.

By 2001, we were almost nine years into a soft market, and there were no real signs that it was going to turn anytime soon. By the insurance industry's estimation, we were at least four years overdue for the market to harden, which would have led to significant and, in my opinion, arbitrary price increases, and all I heard from the industry professionals was this: "Be prepared. The market is starting to harden. These low rates can't last for long."

And so it went.

Then there were the bombings of the World Trade Center and the Pentagon on September 11, 2001. Now, there is no doubt that this was a catastrophic event, the likes of which have never been seen on American soil. But from an insurance standpoint, and particularly from a property casualty standpoint, this was not a catastrophe that should have ushered in the hard market in the insurance industry that came about immediately after these events—especially in the property casualty market.

Much of the loss of life was covered through life insurance. As of this writing, the property claim at the World Trade Center has yet to be resolved, although a federal jury has categorized the event as two occurrences, meaning that the ownership group could collect the limits twice because the policy was written on an occurrence basis.

The losses that ensued from business interruption and loss of revenue coverage were well funded prior to this loss, and therefore should have been a nonfactor. I firmly believe that the insurance industry took this event and used it as an excuse to arbitrarily "harden" the market. The losses were well funded, and although the fallout from 9/11 did result in the bankruptcy of some insurance carriers, these companies can find no fault beyond their own parking lots because of their internal reserve and surplus policies before the event.

Now that the industry has had the opportunity to review the economic fallout from these attacks, these appear to be a consensus of understanding:

- Total economic loss due to the attacks was around $38 billion.

- Insurance losses amounted to roughly 50 percent of that total ($19.1 billion).

- The property damage to the World Trade Center alone was approximately $7 billion of the total

- Much of the losses were covered by life insurance, which would not significantly affect the property casualty side of insurance.

Thus, you are looking at property casualty losses, independent of the WTC loss, which was absorbed by one group of insurers and reinsurers. The insurance losses were less than $10 billion. In contrast to this, the economic effects of Hurricane Katrina are estimated to be in excess of $50 billion. Hurricanes Ivan and Charley in the summer of 2004 have estimated losses of $19 billion. Yet, neither of these events seems to have yet had the impact on the insurance markets that the 9/11 attacks did.

I believe there was a watershed decision made in 1999 that should have put the debate of the hard market to rest. In that year, Congress passed the Financial Services Modernization (Gramm-Leach-Bliley) Act. This act allowed, for the first time, banks to offer insurance products and for insurers to offer banking services through holding companies. This created a synergy between the two industries which allowed both to tap into their customer bases and mine business from the other industry. Banks and insurance companies could offer their clients a one-stop alternative for both insurance and banking.

The result was an increase in competition in the marketplace, which led to consolidation of companies that were too weak to compete in the more dynamic market. The increased competition increased supply for a fairly stable demand, reducing the prices in the marketplace. The increased competition also caused some weaker insurers to lower their qualifications for coverage, which weakened their overall book of business and made them susceptible to the vagaries of the free market. At the same time, it provided a need for coverage in the secondary market that was not being fulfilled at a reasonable price.

These market conditions were becoming evident prior to 2001 and fell back into line fairly quickly after 2001. From an indemnity standpoint, the 9/11 attacks should have been a nonevent but for the insurance industry's need to have an excuse to raise premiums and rid themselves of some bad risks they were forced to take due to the increased competition from FSMA.

Of course, there was one aspect of the 2001 attacks that allowed the industry to get pretty healthy pretty quickly. That was the introduction of terrorism coverage.

Terrorism Risk Insurance Act (TRIA) of 2002

After 9/11, the insurance industry saw that there was a need for terrorist attacks to be funded and covered if and when they occur again. The insurance industry, though, began to exclude terrorism from their policies and refused to insure this risk unless the federal government agreed to back this coverage in cases of a severe and catastrophic loss.

Congress agreed to do this in 2002, and the industry was able to provide this coverage for an additional premium and really no risk, because the federal government agreed to back all but a nominal portion of these claims.

The Terrorism Risk Insurance Program Reauthorization and Extension Act of 2007 extends TRIA until the end of 2014. This extension has been touted as one in which the insurance industry takes on more responsibility for losses, which we in business should see in the form of higher premiums beginning in 2006.

If you really look at it, either allowing the law to sunset at the end of 2005 or extending it as they did is a windfall for the insurance industry. The extension provides for stopgaps once claims hit a certain amount, while the House bill moved to encompass group health into the provisions of the law as well.

Now, think about what would have happened were TRIA allowed to sunset. The insurance industry would no longer have been able to "afford" this coverage without a federal backdrop and would either begin excluding this coverage from its lines of insurance or price it so high as to make it unattractive to potential business customers.

Since the industry began selling this coverage, it has collected hundreds of millions of dollars in premium.

How much cash has actually been paid out for terrorism losses in the United States?

None. Zero.

Yet if the federal law were allowed to expire, the insurers would be allowed to walk away from this coverage with the entire premium without any losses.

Good work if you can get it, and a great way for an allegedly ailing industry to get really healthy really quick.

Tort Reform

Tort reform is a hot issue these days. It was a hot issue yesterday, and it will be a hot issue tomorrow. It seems to have manifested itself in the medical malpractice area, but could probably use some restraints in all areas of tort liability.

That will never happen. The most basic reason for this is that the special interests groups are trying to get the federal government to mandate controls on tort liability. But insurance is controlled by the states.

This issue has been batted around for over one hundred years, and always ends up back in the hands of the states, for better or for worse:

- In 1869, in *Paul v. Virginia,* the U.S. Supreme Court ruled that insurance was not interstate commerce and therefore was not subject to federal regulation.

- In 1890, the Sherman Antitrust Act forbade insurance companies from banding together and colluding to fix prices. This act is still in effect today.

- In 1944, the South-Eastern Underwriters Association (SEUA) decision effectively gave the right to regulate insurance to the federal government after it rendered the decision that the SEUA had conspired to control 90 percent of the insurance business in six states.

- Congress passed the McCarran-Ferguson Act in 1945, which restored state regulation of insurance less than one year after the SEUA decision.

It's fairly obvious that insurance regulation is going to continue to be controlled by the states, and this right has been fiercely protected throughout U.S. history. So, although you will find pockets of state legislation that restrict the awards in tort liability cases, this issue will never get up enough steam to become a federal mandate and will probably be struck down as unconstitutional in deference to states' rights.

This is not the primary reason, though. The real underlying reason is…

Lawyers!

It's so obvious, isn't it? A lawyer sues another party because of their negligence. What does the other party do? They hire a lawyer. Either the other party or its insurance carrier needs legal representation to represent its interests in this action. If the complaining party settles or wins the case, the plaintiff attorney profits. If the defendant wins or loses, the attorney for the defense profits.

If tort reform is passed, who stands to lose the most?

Lawyers!

And most of the folks in Congress, before they became representatives, were…

Lawyers!

Enough said. If all the lawyers are against tort reform, and it would be struck down even were it enacted, it will never happen.

Conclusion

There really is not another book out there in the market that addresses the needs of the business insurance consumer. For as long as there has been insurance, there have been business professionals who have refused to enlighten themselves on the nuances of the insurance trade, and this lack of knowledge adversely affects the bottom line of their businesses. I have seen firsthand how the lack of care and attention can cost companies millions of dollars.

Because insurance and risk management is not a glamour position in the business world, folks like myself toil in relative anonymity, attempting not only to ensure financial stability for our chosen company, but also to educate middle and upper management on the value of such programs.

Yet, here I am. My role is considered in the business community as a "nonrevenue-generating activity." I don't make or provide anything of value that can be sold in the marketplace. So I sit quietly, go about my business, handle all the things no one else wants to deal with, and then go home. I could live with that if it weren't costing business in general and my company in particular *so much money!*

So I offer up this book, and I hope I have been able to educate you to pay more attention to your organization's insurance programs and avoid having all of the money you work so hard to earn fly out the window.

If you remember one thing from this book, remember this:

> *It's your Company.*
> *It's Your Money.*
> *You Can Keep More of It Because...*
> *It's Right There on the Table.*

God bless!
Rick Vassar

PART III
Terms to Know

Glossary

A.M. Best rating. The accepted rating company of an insurer's financial strength.

Actual cash value (ACV). The market value of an asset at the time of the loss less depreciation.

Additional insured. An entity added to a general liability policy as a condition of existing contracts. The additional insured is protected under the terms of the insurance contract.

Admitted carrier. An insurance company licensed to do business in a given state. The insurer is subject to the insurance regulation of its activity in that state. An admitted carrier contributes to state guaranty funds, and, therefore, its insureds have the protection of such a fund if the insurer becomes insolvent.

Adverse selection. The tendency that most insurance is purchased by those most likely to have losses.

Aggregate. The total amount to be paid under the policy during the specified period, no matter how many occurrences. Once the aggregate limits are met under a policy, an insurer will make no more payments.

All risks coverage. Coverage for all loss exposures except for those specifically excluded.

Allocated loss expense (ALE). These are loss expenses that relate directly to a specific claim. An ALE is generally noted in the last column of a loss run, but is usually not included in the total (incurred loss) calculation.

Alternative risk financing. A non-insurance risk-financing technique (e.g., hold harmless agreements, indemnity agreements, hedging, retention, and contractual transfer).

Annual minimum premium. The minimum premium to be paid, regardless of audit results. If the audit comes out higher, you pay the additional premium. If the audited premium is lower, the insured is not refunded the difference.

Assigning markets. The process brokers insist upon in which each broker is allowed to go to certain carriers exclusively to market your account when you renew your insurance.

Auditable policy. Commercial policy based on unit estimates (e.g., gross revenue or payroll) that are then audited after the policy ends to determine the actual premium.

Bare-bones policy. A policy with very few endorsements or additional coverage.

Boilerplate. A standard (bare-bones) contract.

Broker of record. Broker who represents your interests with the insurance carriers.

Business continuity. An organization's ability to continue operating after a loss.

Business income coverage (BIC). Coverage under a property-package policy to compensate a company for lost income in addition to the cost of repair.

Capacity. Total amount of coverage an insurer has the ability to write. This is based on a capacity ratio that measures the premium-to-surplus ratio (an amount after which the value of an insurer's assets exceeds their liabilities).

Captive insurer. An insurance company formed for the exclusive use of the parent company.

Claims made coverage form. A claim made during the policy period or any extended reporting period. This policy defines the time period in which a claim can be reported.

Classification of operations. The class under which an employee's work is categorized in a workers' compensation policy, using the Scopes Manual as a guide. The riskier the work classification, the higher the cost.

Coinsurance provision. In property policies, a provision in which the insured must keep the limits within a specified percentage of the actual replacement value to collect the entire limits of the policy.

Collision coverage. Covers the insured vehicle for physical damage due to an accident/incident, usually subject to a deductible.

Combined single limit (CSL). The maximum the insurer will pay for a single auto liability loss as opposed to breaking down limits to a per-person, per-occurrence and property damage basis.

Compensatory damages. Damages intended to reimburse the injured party for the loss, including medical bills (specials), loss of income, property, and pain and suffering.

Composite auto policy. An auto policy in which all vehicles in a fleet are afforded the same coverage. Pricing is based on the total value of all vehicles and the additional coverage elected by the insured.

Comprehensive (comp) coverage. Losses to an insured's vehicles incurred as a result of forces beyond the insured's control—also referred to as "act of God" losses, including wind, hail, and fire.

Consent to settle provision. Generally found in professional liability policies, it gives the insurer the right to settle a case without permission of the insured.

Contingent business income exposures. Coverage under a property/package policy to compensate for the loss of income due to supplier's inability to provide a product or service essential to the production of your product or service.

Contracts of adhesion. Contract written by one party and accepted as written by the other party to the contract without modification. Insurance contracts/ policies are contracts of adhesion.

Corporate reimbursement coverage. Under a directors and officers policy, this coverage reimburses the organization for any losses covered under the policy.

Cost of risk. Amount of cost incurred by an organization to insulate itself from losses. These costs include insurance premiums, retained losses, risk and claims administration, outside services (TPAs, litigation, administrative costs), fees and taxes, security instruments such as letters of credit or bonds, and soft costs, such as replacing damaged and disabled vehicles, temporary replacement of injured employee.

Cover. The contract of insurance.

Coverage form. Form in which coverage is offered, generally either on an "occurrence basis" (if the loss occurs during the policy period) or a "claims made basis," which limits losses to those reported during the policy period and a specified extended reporting period.

Current expensing. Paying losses under self-insured programs as they are incurred.

'Damages to premises rented to you' limit. Coverage under the general liability policy that covers for premises rented for seven days or less.

Declaration page. Evidences the insured's coverage as well as special provisions to the specific entity asking for such evidence.

Deductible. The first layer of a loss, which the insured must pay before the insurer begins coverage. The insurer retains control of the claim settlement.

Defendant. The party from which the injured party seeks compensation for tort (noncontractual) liability due to the defendant's negligence.

Direct coverage (D&O). The coverage for losses due to the negligent act of a director or officer that the company is not legally obligated to pay.

Direct employees. Employees who participate directly in the manufacture of the product or the delivery of the service.

Drafting authority. The authority given by the insured to a third party administrator (adjusting company) or broker in alternative financing situations to settle claims without the input of the insured.

Drive other vehicle coverage. This extends coverage to named individuals who do not own a personal vehicle but who have access to a company vehicle. This coverage is intended to cover the named individual under the auto policy in any vehicle he or she drives. This is generally afforded to owners and key executives.

Drop down coverage. Excess or umbrella insurer that steps up to pay losses under the underlying policy, when the underlying insurer becomes insolvent.

Earned premium. The amount of premium that has been used during the policy period. If premium is paid in excess of the portion of the policy period (written premium) that has expired, that portion of the premium is considered unearned premium. Earned premium is an asset to the insurer whereas unearned premium is considered a liability until earned.

Electronic data processing (EDP) floater. Provides protection from the loss of electronic data due to a power loss or breach of the organization system or network.

Employee Retirement Income Security Act (ERISA). Federal law that provides guidelines for employee benefit programs for employers doing business in multiple states.

Employer's liability coverage. This coverage extends the limits of coverage as well as the scope of coverage afforded under workers' compensation insurance, which is statutorily mandated.

Employment practices liability insurance (EPLI). Coverage to protect the organization from claims arising from employment issues such as sexual harassment, discrimination, and wrongful termination.

Endorsements. Amendments to the standard contract that adds, clarifies, or restricts coverage.

Environmental impairment liability (EIL). Compensation for first and third party claims arising from an environment-impairing incident for which the organization is found liable.

Equipment breakdown insurance. Coverage under a package/property policy, used to compensate the company for an economic loss due to the breakdown of a key piece of equipment.

Equipment floater. Insures mobile equipment away from premises.

Erode. Typically used in alternative financing in which the insured pays losses up to a certain threshold. The payment of a loss serves to "erode" the amount of the self-insured portion of the policy

Evidence of coverage. The insurance policy. It can also refer to the declaration (dec) page, which evidences a company's coverage.

Excess carrier. Insurer used to extend policy limits. The excess carrier sits above the primary policy limits for a specific underlying policy.

Exclusions. Losses specifically excluded from a policy's coverage.

Experience modification rate (EMR). *See* Mod rate.

Fidelity bond. Security that guarantees against the dishonest acts of an employee; also provides indemnification required by ERISA for those benefit plans subject to ERISA requirements.

Fire legal liability limit. This coverage, under the general liability policy, covers fire loss to property rented or occupied by the insured with the owner's permission.

First-dollar coverage. Traditional, guaranteed cost insurance in which a premium is paid to an insurer and all covered losses are paid by the insurer.

First party claim. A claim against your own policy.

Flat policy. A policy in which the premium paid up front is the total amount of the policy and not subject to audit.

Floaters. Policies that covers property that can be moved from one location to another for both transportation perils and perils affecting property at a fixed location.

Forms schedule. The page that shows the documents that change or amend the basic language of the standard policy.

Frequency. The number of losses that an organization incurs during a specified period.

Funded reserves. Cash set aside to pay losses that occur through a self-insured plan.

General aggregate limit. The maximum insurance afforded under one policy.

Guaranteed cost coverage. Traditional first-dollar coverage in which a premium is paid to an insurer and all covered losses are paid by the insurer (*see* first-dollar coverage).

Hard market. When the entire insurance market experiences an escalation of premium costs.

Incurred but not reported (IBNR). Those losses that have occurred during the policy period but have not yet been reported and are usually included as an estimate by formula by the insurer when valuing a policy's loss history.

Incurred losses. The total of paid claims plus reserves.

In-house employee. One who works for the company, and is not independent, such as an auditor or attorney.

Inland marine insurance. Covers land-based risks related to transportation and communication.

Investigative adjusting. A claims department or third party administrator that will commit resources to examining a claim to determine the best possible outcome, instead of "processing" a claim for payment.

"Law of large numbers." Statistical term that states that the more frequency you have, the better your ability to predict potential future results.

Liability. Any legally enforceable act or obligation.

Limits of insurance. The total amount of coverage afforded under an insurance policy.

Liquidity. The ability to turn a financial instrument into cash.

Long tail. A claim that requires a long settlement period.

Loss. The reduction in the value of an insured's property caused by a covered peril.

Loss exposure. A hazard that has the potential for loss.

Loss prevention. A risk-control measure designed to reduce the frequency (number) of losses.

Loss reduction. A risk-control measure designed to reduce the severity (amount) of claims.

Minimum earned premium at inception. The minimum amount of premium to be paid if the policy is cancelled as early as the day after it is initiated.

Mod rate. Experience modification rate (EMR) measures a company's workers' compensation losses tied to the industry average and assigns a rate that is then applied to the insured's work comp premium. The industry average is 1.00. A mod rate above 1.00 indicates a surcharge, and a mod rate below 1.00 prompts a credit.

Monopolistic states. States that do not allow competition from outside insurers and instead provide their own structure and rules for workers' compensation.

Named driver auto policy. Auto policy in which the drivers are scheduled instead of the autos. Generally used in large fleets in which drivers regularly switch vehicles. Because this policy will not satisfy the auto insurance mandatory coverage laws, it is generally used to supplement and protect a master policy with a high self-insured retention.

National Council on Compensation Insurance, Inc. (NCCI). The accepted governing body for workers' compensation in most states.

Non-admitted carrier. An insurer not licensed to do business in the state but who is allowed to provide coverage as a "surplus lines" insurer.

Nuisance claim. A claim that has little or no merit yet must be defended.

Occupational injuries. Injuries that occur on the job.

Occurrence form. Covers claims arising out of occurrences that take place during the policy period.

Occurrence limit. The total amount of coverage afforded for one incident.

Other states (or limited other states) endorsement. Insurance providing workers' compensation coverage for temporary work done in another state, subject to state statutory restrictions.

Outsourcing. Paying a third party to handle a certain responsibility on behalf of the organization.

Paid claims. The amount on a loss run in which payment has been made.

Pain and suffering. Damages awarded to compensate the injured party for costs which cannot be quantified.

Per-occurrence basis. The total amount (limit) an insurance policy will pay for any one loss.

Personal and advertising injury limits. Under a general liability policy, this covers libel, slander, false imprisonment, and other intentional acts.

Personal injury protection (PIP). Medical payments afforded in addition to liability coverage under auto policies. This coverage is mandatory in some states and is generally afforded regardless of fault.

Physical damage coverage. Coverage afforded to protect an insured's assets from physical loss.

Plaintiff. The party alleging harm due to the negligence of another party.

Policy period. The specified amount of time the insurance policy covers, generally one year.

Premium. The agreed-upon price for the specified insurance coverage.

Premium basis. An estimate of the exposure of a policy for purposes of determining an initial premium. This is also used to determine the actual premium due upon audit of the policy.

Processors. Adjusting companies that settle claims with little or no investigation.

Products-completed operations aggregate limit. Coverage under general liability that insulates the insured from losses that occur due to negligent construction or operation.

Punitive damages. Damages awarded to the injured party intended to punish the negligent party due to willful or wanton negligence.

Qualified self-insurer. An entity licensed and bonded by a public entity as a self-insurer by proving it has met minimum financial requirements.

Reinsurance. A source of coverage used by insurers to reduce risk and increase capacity.

Reserve. On a loss run, the estimated amount of future payouts for a loss.

Retained losses. Losses an organization pays itself (in-house).

Retrospectively rated insurance plans. Insurance policy in which an insured receives premium rebates if losses remain below a specified threshold on certain anniversaries after the expiration of the policy. This can be done on a paid loss basis but is generally offered on an incurred loss basis.

Rider. A document that amends an insurance policy or certificate.

Scheduled auto policy. An auto policy that covers only the vehicles that are specifically named.

Scopes Manual (Scope of Basic Manual Classifications). Manual that provides a detailed narrative of each employment classification for workers' compensation coverage. The manual is issued by the National Council on Compensation Insurance, Inc. (NCCI).

Self-insured retention (SIR). An insurance policy in which the insured agrees to pay losses up to a specified threshold while retaining control of the claim until the SIR is eroded.

Severity. The amount or size of each loss.

Slip and fall coverage. Commercial general liability policies are sometimes referred to as slip and fall insurance due to the frequency of these specific types of claims.

Special damages. Actual losses incurred by an injured party in a loss.

Stand-alone policy. A policy that covers a specific loss exposure; specialized coverage.

State guaranty fund. A fund that protects the insured from the insolvency of an admitted carrier.

Stop loss. The total amount to be paid by the insured, generally on an aggregate basis, before coverage kicks in.

Strict liability. A situation in which the insured is liable for a loss regardless of negligence or fault.

Sunset. Provision that allows an obligation to expire.

Surplus lines broker. A broker licensed to sell coverage from non-admitted carriers if certain guidelines are met.

Third party administrator (TPA). An adjusting company hired to manage and settle self-insured losses.

Third party liability claim. A claim made by one party that believes it suffered a loss for which another party is responsible.

Tolerable risk. A risk that the organization feels it can take to conduct its business.

Tort. Any civil wrong that is not a breach of contract.

Total advance premium. Agreed upon premium prior to the policy's existence. This premium is subject to audit after the policy period ends.

Underground storage tank (UST) coverage. Protects a company from losses arising from underground storage facilities, such as gas and oil tanks.

Underwriter. The individual who determines the pricing of a policy for the insurer.

Underwriting. Process of classifying and selecting risks and applying appropriate rates.

Unearned premium. The portion of written premium that has not been "used up" (the amount of time which has not elapsed on the policy).

Unfunded reserves. Anticipated funds that will be needed to fund retained losses in the future. Unfunded reserves are generally recorded as a notation on financial statements and thus not recorded as a liability.

Uninsured motorist (UM) coverage. Coverage to protect the insured from losses incurred by an uninsured negligent party. This coverage is mandatory in many states and is under the liability portion of the auto policy. For this reason, first party physical damage losses are covered without a deductible incurred by the insured in most states.

Unmodified premium. Under a workers' compensation policy, it is the premium before any discount, surcharge, or mod rate is applied.

Workers' compensation (work comp) coverage. Coverage for the employee for work-related injuries regardless of fault.

Wrongful acts. A negligent act, error and omission, breach of duty, misstatement, or misleading statement.

Index

actual cash value (ACV), 155
additional insured, 123, 155
adjuster
    dealing with, 64–65, 66 i
    nformation about, 64
    job, 66
    life of, 66–69
adjusting companies
    agreement with, 89
    authority of, 89
    function of, 86, 87
    investigative, 87
    selecting, 87
    settlements and, 86–87
admitted carrier, 138, 155
adverse selection, 155
aggregate, 155
allocated loss expense (ALE), 155
all risks coverage, 121, 155
alternative risk financing, 155
    business, 81–82
    managing, 82–83
    personal, 80–81
A.M. Best rating, 155
annual minimum premium, 124, 156
assigning markets, 40–41, 156
audit
    appealing, 102
    automobile, 101
    general liability, 100
    overtime, 99
    package, 98–99
    payroll and, 99–100
    preparing for, 97, 101
    workers' compensation, 97–98
auditable policy, 124, 156

auditor
    classifying employees, 100
    dealing with, 97
    information for, 99
    mistakes by, 102
    objectives of, 96
auto insurance
    commercial, 106–107
    composite, 101
    coverage, 108–110
    discounts, 111–112
    drivers, 111–112, 113
    for fleets, 107
    policies, 110–111, 113
    policy explanation, 108
    premiums, 101
    scheduled, 101
    types of, 106–107
auto liability, 105, 106
automobile audits, 101

bailment, xvi
banks, 32, 147
bare-bones policy, 111, 156
binder, 125
boilerplate, 156
broker
    assigning markets to, 41
    bidding, 48
    caveats about, 35 167
    commercial, 43
    competition among, 42
    finding, 23
    marketing considerations, 45
    of record, 39, 156
    relationship with, 43–44
    reliance on, 30
    and renewing contracts, 40–41
    and sales, 26
    selecting, 42–43
    submitting quotes, 48–49
    surplus line, 138
    using several, 41–42
brokerage firms, 43

business
    alternative risk financing, 81–82
    continuity, 156
    income coverage (BIC), 120, 156
    small. *See* small business success, 18
capacity, 156
captive insurer, 81, 156
claims
    adjusters, 61, 63
     administration, 62
    age of, 73
    categories of, 83
    collecting, 70, 71
    costs of, 88
    deductible program, 85
    defending, 70
    department, 66–67
    handling, 63
    impact of, 23
    injured employees, 135. *See also*
        workers' compensation
    investigating, 138
    large, 90
    liabilities, 64–65
    limits, 137
    lingering, 129
    "long tail," 129
    made coverage form, 123, 156
    nuisance, 140
    package, 69
    parties, 62
    payment, 90
    preparing for, 63
    procedures for, 89
    reporting, 123, 133
    and retro plans, 83–84
    self-funding, 82–83, 91
    self-insurance and, 77–78
    settling, 90, 140
    size of, 73–74
    subjectivity of, 70
    subrogation, 65
    types of, 61
    workers' compensation, 130–131
classification of
operations, 131, 156
coinsurance provision, 114, 116–117, 157
    collection
        agencies, 72–74

strategy, 71
collision coverage, 156
combined single limit (CSL), 157
commercial general liability coverage, 126,
    127–128
commercial insurance, 23
compensatory damages, 157
composite auto policy, 157
comprehensive (comp) coverage, 157
confidentiality agreement, 54
consent to settle provision, 157
contingency basis, 54
contingent business income exposure, 120,
    157
contracts of adhesion, 157
corporate reimbursement coverage, 157
cost of risk, 157–158
counsel, 53
cover, 158
coverage forms, 123, 158
crimes, 142–143
current expensing, 158
customer goodwill, 43
damages to premises rented to you limit,
    123, 158
declaration page, 123, 158
deductible, 158
deductible programs, 84–85
defendant, 158
direct employees, 158
directors and officers (D&O) coverage, 142,
    158
disability, 129
downsizing, 67
drafting authority, 89, 158
drive other vehicle coverage, 158
drop down, 139, 159
drug-free workplace (DFWP), 112
duplication, 120
earned premium, 79, 159
    electronic data processing (EDP)
        floater, 159
    Employee Retirement Income Security
        Act (ERISA), 159
employees
    checking history of, 112
    classifying, 98–99, 100, 131–132
    crimes by, 142–143
    disabled, 129
    driving considerations, 106

drug testing, 112
injured, 129, 130, 133–134, 135
traveling, 134
employer's liability, 131, 159
employment practices liability coverage, 137
employment practices liability insurance
(EPLI), 126–127, 140–141, 159
endorsements, 126, 127, 159
environmental impairment liability (EIL),
143, 159
environmental liability, 143
equipment, 120
equipment breakdown insurance, 120, 159
equipment floater, 159
erode, 159
evidence of coverage, 160
excess carrier, 160
exclusions, 126, 140–141, 148, 160
experience modification rate (EMR), 132–
133, 160
Fair Credit Reporting Act, 112
fidelity bond, 160
Financial Services Modernization Act, 32
fire legal liability limit, 123, 160
first-dollar coverage, 160
first party claim, 160
flat policy, 160
floaters, 160
forms schedule, 126, 160
frequency, 160
funded reserves, 82, 160
general aggregate limit, 123, 160
general liability
commercial, 127–128
coverage, 123
general liability (GL)
policy amending, 126
audits, 100
coverage, 123, 126–127
endorsements, 127
exclusions, 126–127
need for, 122
premium, 124
requirements, 100
Gramm-Leach-Bliley Act, 32, 147
guaranteed cost coverage, 161
hard market, 39, 145–146, 161
hostile work environment, 126
human resources, 30
hurricanes, 147

incurred but not reported (IBNR), 161
incurred losses, 161
in-house counsel, 53
in-house employee, 161
inland marine insurance, 120, 161
insolvency, 138, 139
instincts, 1–2
insurance
additional coverage, 136
adjusters, 64. *See also* adjuster
alternative risk financing, 78
automobile. *See* auto insurance
buying, 27
carrier, 84
claims. *See* claims
costs, 22–23, 35, 42, 133
deciding on, 137
equipment breakdown, 120–121
guaranteed cost, 80
limits of, 123–124
and losses, 35, 126–127
marketing products, 32
minimizing costs, 76
miscellaneous coverage, 138
mod rate and, 133
paperwork, 30
policies. *See* policies
pricing, 48
professional liability, 140
proof of, 139–140
reason for, 136–137
regulators, 79
reinsurance, 79–80
retro plans, 83–84
self-, 76–79, 90–91
shopping for, 44–45
small business, 15
state regulations, 131
subrogation, 65
terrorism coverage, 31
traditional, 78–79, 80
traveling employees, 135
understanding, 5, 23–24
insurance companies
banking services, 32, 147
downsizing, 67
employee classification, 98
licensing, 138
limits of sales, 79
maximum payment, 123–124

valuing property, 118–119
insurance industry
    and the banking industry, 32
    commercial, 23
     investments, 32
    jobs in, 9
    knowledge of, 21
    terrorism and, 31
insurance programs
    deductible, 84–85
    marketing, 45
    preparations, 92
    self-insured retention, 86
investigative adjusting, 161
land, 115
"law of large numbers," 161
lawsuits
    confidentiality agreement, 54
    medical bills, 56
    reasons for, 55
    settling, 54, 55–56
lawyers
    caveats about, 52, 53
    relationship with, 54
    and risk management, 51
    tort reform and, 149–150
    workers' compensation claims and,
        131
    young, 72–73
liability, 161
    claims, 64–65
    employer, 131
    employment practices, 140–141
    environmental, 143
    excess, 139
    limits, 139
    professional errors and omissions, 140
    tort, 55
limits, 26–27
    advertising injury, 123
    of insurance, 123–124, 161
    liability, 139
    occurrence, 123
    personal injury, 123
    products-completed operations
        aggregate, 124
liquidity, 161
litigation, 54
long tail, 161
loss, 161

damaged location, 120
and driving, 112
environmental, 143
expenses, 90
exposure, 139, 161
funding anticipated, 81–82
history, 47
incurred, 84
mitigating, 36
paying, 76
prevention, 161
products, 120
property, 117
reduction, 162
reporting, 72
runs, 47
services, 120
settling, 86
size of, 35
stop, 119
substantiating, 69
unanticipated, 126

market
    assigning, 40–41
    hard, 39, 145–146
    soft, 146
marketing
    information, 45–47 insurance and,
        139–140 presentation, 45, 47
minimum earned premium at inception,
    125, 162
modification rate (mod rate), 36, 132–133,
    162
monopolistic states, 162
named driver auto policy, 162
National Council on Compensation
    Insurance, Inc. (NCCI), 36, 162
negligence, 123
non-admitted carrier, 138–139, 162
nuisance claim, 162
occupational injuries, 162
occurrence form, 123, 162
occurrence limit, 123, 162
other states endorsement, 162
outside counsel, 53
outsourcing, 163
overtime, 99
paid amount plus reserve, 86
paid claims, 163

pain and suffering, 163
payroll
    and audits, 99–100
    estimating, 100, 125
per-occurrence basis, 163
personal alternative risk financing, 80–81
personal and advertising injury limits, 163
personal injury protection (PIP), 163
physical damage coverage, 163
plaintiff, 163
policies
    auditable, 124, 156
    bare-bones, 111, 156
    brokers and, 41–42
    canceling, 125
    composite auto, 107–108, 110
    cost of, 124
    crime, 142–143
    equipment, 120
    floaters, 120
    general liability, 100
    history, 47
    information, 120
    named driver, 113
    packages, 121
    period, 123, 163
    property/package. *See* property/
      package coverage
    reading, 24–25
    renewal date, 99
    renewing, 40–41, 98
    scheduled auto, 106–107, 110
    stand-alone, 126
    surplus lines, 138
    umbrella, 139
premium, 163
    auto insurance policies, 101
    basis, 132, 163
    calculating, 124, 132
    composite auto policies, 107–108
    deductible program, 85
    discount, 132
    earned, 79
    estimating basis, 125
    forfeited, 126
    general liability policy, 100, 124
    and market conditions, 145–146
    minimum, 124–125
    unmodified, 132
    workers' compensation and, 98

pricing, 48
processors, 163
products-completed operations aggregate
    limit, 163
professional errors and omissions (E&O)
    liability, 140
property
    appraisals, 117, 118–119
    bailment, xvi
    coinsurance, 116–117
    coverage. *See* property/package
      coverage
    mobile equipment, 120
    at other locations, 120
    overinsuring, 116
    owned, 115
    personal, 119
    real, 119
    in transit, 120
    value of, 115, 116
property/package coverage, 114
    appraisals and, 115, 117
    coinsurance clause, 116–117
    exclusions, 121
    land, 115
punitive damages, 163
qualified self-insurer, 89, 164
reinsurance, 79–80, 164
reserve, 164
retained losses, 164
retrospectively rated insurance plans, 81,
    83– 84, 164
rider, 164
risk management, 3
    duplication, 120
    evolution of, 29–32
    and lawyers, 51
    need for, 29
    process, 32–34
risk manager
    function of, xv, 7, 24
    and lawsuits, 53–54
risk retention groups, 81
rollover account, 44
schedule, 120
scheduled auto policy, 106–107, 164
Scopes manual, 98, 132, 164
self-insurance, 76–79
self-insurance pools, 81
self-insured retention (SIR), 81, 86, 90, 164

Services Modernization Act, 147
severity, 164
sexual harassment, 126–127, 140
slip and fall coverage, 122, 164
small business
    developing, 17
    flexibility, 17
    insuring, 15–16, 18
    start-up, 14–15, 16
soft market, 146
special damages, 164
stand-alone policy, 126, 164
state guaranty fund, 138, 164
statutory self-insurer, 89
stop loss, 119, 165
strict liability, 165
subrogation, 65
sunset, 31, 165
surplus lines, 138, 165
terrorism, 31, 146–147
Terrorism Risk Insurance Act (TRIA), 148
third-party administrator (TPA), 77, 165.
    See also adjusting companies
third-party liability claim, 165
tolerable risk, 165
tort liability, 55, 165
tort reform, 148–149
total advance premium, 124, 165
umbrella liability, 139
underground storage tanks (UST) coverage,
    165
underwriters, 27, 39, 165
unearned premium, 165
unfunded reserves, 165
uninsured motorist (UM) coverage, 165–
    166
unmodified premium, 166
workers' compensation (work comp)
    and employee classification, 132
    exemptions, 129
    need for, 129–130
    policy, 134–135
    states and, 134
    strategies, 133–134
workers' compensation insurance, 166
    audits, 97–98
    fraudulent claims, 130–131
    need for, 18
    premium pricing, 98
    purpose of, 130, 131

state requirements, 36
wrongful acts, 142, 166

CPSIA information can be obtained at www.ICGtesting.com
Printed in the USA
268535BV00001B/27/P

9 781605 280202